KU-529-611

FOCUS ON

IELTS

TEACHER'S BOOK

Longman

SUE O'CONNELL

Pearson Education Limited
Edinburgh Gate, Harlow
Essex CM20 2JE, England
and Associated Companies throughout the world

www.longman.com

© Sue O'Connell 2002

The right of Sue O'Connell to be identified as the
author of this Work has been asserted by her in
accordance with the Copyright, Designs and Patents
Act 1988.

All rights reserved; no part of this publication may be
reproduced, stored in a retrieval system, or transmitted
in any form or by any means, electronic, mechanical,
photocopying, recording, or otherwise without the prior
written permission of the Publishers.

First published 2002

Set in 10/12pt Times New Roman

Printed in Spain by Gráficas Estella

ISBN 0 582 44772 0

Designed by Jennifer Coles

Project managed by Catriona Watson-Brown

Cover photograph © Stone

▶ Contents

▶ Introduction

Focus on IELTS is a complete course which provides thorough preparation for the Listening and Speaking modules and the Academic Reading and Writing modules of the IELTS Test. It contains essential information and advice about IELTS modules and tasks, comprehensive exam preparation and a useful end section providing supplementary practice material.

The course is designed to build students' confidence and proficiency through systematic skills development and graded exam practice. Texts and tasks have been chosen to motivate, highlight key strategies and also encourage students to play an active role in their own learning. The optional practice in the *Key language bank* and the *Writing practice bank* is suitable for individual or class use, and allows teachers maximum flexibility in matching the material to different course formats and in tailoring the course to suit mixed-ability classes and to meet specific needs.

Key features of the course

- **Exam briefing** boxes focus on each module and introduce key task-types.

- **Task approach** sections outline key strategies for tackling individual questions.

- **Reminder** sections act as a memory aid for key exam strategies.

- Regular **Error Hit Lists**, based on the *Longman Learner's Corpus*, help students to identify and correct typical usage mistakes.

- A **Practice test** provides an opportunity to work through a complete test at the end of the course.

- The **Key language bank** provides extra practice in key areas of grammar and vocabulary. Relevant exercises are signposted throughout the units.

- The **Writing practice bank** provides guided answers for selected questions, together with additional writing topics. Relevant exercises are signposted in the units.

This book provides detailed teaching notes, full keys to exercises and scripts for the recordings.

Structure

The book begins with an *Overview* of the exam. This provides a summary of the four modules in the IELTS Test, followed by detailed information about the tasks students can expect, and the assessment criteria which are used in marking each paper.

This is followed by the twenty units, divided into pairs under ten general topic headings. Odd-numbered units

(1, 3, etc.) focus mainly on reading, while even-numbered units (2, 4, etc.) focus mainly on listening and writing. There is also a variety of speaking practice in both odd- and even-numbered units. Thus all the key components of the IELTS Test are covered in each pair of units.

Each unit begins with a box outlining the main practice activities and showing how they relate to the exam, followed by a *Lead-in* section, which explores students' awareness of the topic and topic vocabulary. In addition to reading, listening, writing and speaking practice, other regular features include vocabulary development, pronunciation practice, *Spot the error* tasks and *Error Hit Lists*. For a full description of the unit-by-unit contents, see the *Map of the book* on pages 2 and 3 of the Student's Book.

The end section of the book contains a complete IELTS *Practice test* and a range of supplementary practice material in the *Key language bank* and the *Writing practice bank*. There are also *Answer keys* to selected exercises in the units and to the *Key language* and *Writing practice bank* exercises.

On the final page, there is an index of the main structural and vocabulary items covered in the book and also a complete list of items included in the *Error Hit Lists*.

How to use the course

The material has been designed to be as flexible as possible so that the time needed to work through the course can be expanded or contracted, depending on the level of the students and the contact hours available. Similarly, students can do more or less work outside class depending on their circumstances and individual needs.

Fast-track route

The minimum time needed to complete the course is about 60 hours. In this case, some of the material from the *Focus on vocabulary* and *Focus on writing* sections will need to be set for homework. It may also be helpful if students tackle some of the longer reading tasks before the lesson so that class time can be most productively spent in task analysis. Students will also need to use the *Key language bank* and the *Writing practice bank* in their own time as self-access resources.

More extended courses

If time is not at a premium and most of the work (including relevant supplementary practice exercises) is done in class time, the material could easily occupy 100+ hours.

The *Overview* section provides an appropriate starting point for the course by giving students a clear indication of the goal they are aiming to reach. This section can be referred to regularly as the course progresses and as students become more concerned about the exact requirements of the IELTS test. Each module of the exam and each main task-type is introduced in an *Exam briefing* box, while *Task approach* sections outline strategies for tackling individual questions. The course, like the IELTS exam itself, is graded so that texts and tasks get more difficult as students progress.

At this level, and with an exam as challenging as IELTS, it's particularly important to capitalise on what students can do for themselves. For this reason, students should be encouraged to take responsibility for their own learning by making effective use of good dictionaries and grammar books, as well as resources in the book such as *Spot the error* sections, where they can record their own most common mistakes, the *Error Hit Lists*, which they should study systematically, and the *Key language bank* and *Writing practice bank*, which they can use for individualised practice.

Unit contents

Lead-ins

The *Lead-in* activities include a wide range of discussion topics, quizzes, vocabulary development and problem-solving tasks. They also feature a number of pronunciation exercises which focus on aspects of word stress and sounds, and are relevant not only to students' speaking skills, but also to their listening skills. The *Lead-in* sections serve as an introduction to the topic and a foundation for the activities in the unit. They also allow students to share experience or knowledge they may have, to practise a variety of communicative skills, and to extend their range of topic vocabulary.

Focus on reading

One of the main challenges of the Academic Reading module of the IELTS test is the length of the passages, and it's important that students have plenty of exposure to extended texts in order to develop the skills and confidence needed to deal with them. For this reason, the ten main texts are an accurate reflection of IELTS requirements in terms of content and length. On very intensive courses, this may mean that some reading tasks have to be set for homework. However, there are also a number of shorter texts with tasks designed to practise specific reading skills, which can easily be completed in class time.

The reading texts represent a wide variety of styles and approaches, and sources include books, newspapers, magazines and journals, as well as the Internet. A full range of reading skills are practised, including prediction, skimming/scanning, sampling a text and distinguishing fact from opinion. Each of the main exam task-types, such as completion, matching and

True/False/Does Not Say, is introduced in *Exam briefing* boxes, while clear strategies for dealing with individual questions are set out in *Task approach* sections.

Focus on writing

There is thorough preparation for both tasks in the Academic Writing module, and the skills required are built up from sentence level, with an emphasis on appropriate linking and clear paragraphing. Each task is introduced in an *Exam briefing* box, and there is advice on approaching specific topics in the *Task approach* sections.

For Task 1, students are trained in interpreting information from a wide variety of diagrams, including graphs, charts and tables, and they are also familiarised with the other possible topics (describing objects and processes and explaining how something works). In addition, there is step-by-step practice in producing an effective answer for Task 2, including analysing the question, structuring an argument, beginning and ending, presenting supporting points and writing summarising sentences.

The *Writing practice bank* contains gapped model answers for selected tasks and also additional writing topics.

Focus on listening

The twenty listening texts provide balanced coverage of the four sections of the Listening module and represent a wide variety of speech situations, both formal and informal. The recordings follow the IELTS practice of featuring several varieties of English, including American, Australian, British, Canadian, Irish and New Zealand. The scripts are reproduced at the end of this book.

There are introductions to the four sections of the test and to general task-types such as completion tasks (e.g. completing notes or a summary) and transcoding tasks (e.g. labelling a plan or chart) in *Exam briefing* boxes, while clear strategies for dealing with individual questions are set out in the *Task approach* sections.

Focus on speaking

Students need a wide range of speaking skills in order to do well in the Speaking module. They have to be able to talk about familiar personal matters and general topics in Parts 1 and 2, as well as discussing more abstract issues in Part 3. Among other things, they may need to provide information, express and justify opinions and preferences, compare and contrast, and speculate. In doing so, they must demonstrate fluency and coherence, an adequate range of vocabulary and grammar, and acceptable pronunciation.

This is a tall order, requiring thorough preparation in terms of both language and confidence. For this reason, the book provides ample opportunity for motivating oral practice, not only in the *Focus on speaking* sections, but also in *Lead-ins* and elsewhere. Early units feature a wide variety of speaking activities involving pair or group discussion. Later units move to more exam-focused practice leading to a complete practice interview in Unit 20.

Each of the three parts of the Speaking module is introduced in an *Exam briefing* box, while *Task approach* sections outline exam strategies such as the use of mindmaps in preparing for Part 2. General topics for Parts 1 and 2 include personal interests and goals, visits to cultural attractions and memories of schooldays, while more abstract topics for Part 3 include urban problems, water issues, predicting the future and tourism.

Focus on vocabulary

Students at this level need vocabulary practice in two main areas. Firstly, they must be able to cope with unknown vocabulary, particularly the wide and unpredictable range they will meet in academic reading texts. The key skills here are the ability to identify expressions which are crucial to understanding and to make intelligent guesses as to meaning. Secondly, students need an adequate working vocabulary with which to express themselves clearly on issues ranging from the personal and familiar to the more abstract and perhaps contentious.

Both these areas are addressed in the *Focus on vocabulary* sections. Exercises such as those on derived adjectives and nouns train students in working out the meanings of unknown words, and there is an emphasis throughout on systematic vocabulary-building through the use of word families and other techniques. Other aspects covered include word partners, dependent prepositions and compound nouns. In addition, there are exercises related to writing tasks such as the use of linking expressions and ways of introducing examples.

Students at this level are often anxious about their perceived limitations in terms of vocabulary and are keen to work on this area. For such students, there is a range of optional additional vocabulary practice in the *Key language bank*.

Spot the error

These exercises require students to identify and correct the kind of errors frequently made by learners when writing or speaking about the topic in question. They are a way of encouraging students to make a habit of checking their own work and of learning from their mistakes, since answers and explanations can usually be found in the *Error Hit Lists*. They also provide a useful opportunity for students to systematically record and hopefully eliminate their own most frequent mistakes.

Error Hit Lists

There are ten *Error Hit Lists*, one at the end of each pair of units. These draw on the *Longman Learner's*

Corpus and target the most common errors of grammar or vocabulary relevant to the topic or tasks in the units. Examples include the use of *nevertheless* and the difference between *possibility* and *opportunity* or between *economic, economical* and *financial*.

Error Hit Lists are intended mainly as an active learning resource for students, and it's worth taking time at the beginning of the course to explain exactly what they are and how students can make best use of them. In all, there are 38 language points covering around 90 separate expressions. If students make a point of studying each *Error Hit List* conscientiously and revising them as necessary as the course progresses, they should be able to eliminate a significant number of the most common and predictable errors from their written and spoken English. To encourage this process, it would be helpful to include occasional spot checks and other revision work based on the *Error Hit Lists* in class.

There is a complete list of points covered in the *Error Hit Lists* on page 223 of the Student's Book.

Practice banks

The two practice banks contain supplementary activities which can be used in a number of ways, depending on the time available and students' needs. With lower-level students on more extended courses, you may choose to include most of these exercises in class time. With higher-level students on intensive courses, the exercises can be treated purely as self-access resources. In all other cases, they can be used as and when the need arises, for example for homework, for revision/remedial teaching, to meet the needs of a specific student, or, in the case of vocabulary tasks, as convenient 'fillers' between other segments of a lesson.

All the *Key language* and *Writing practice* exercises are cross-referenced to the relevant unit.

- The *Key language bank* contains 27 supplementary exercises focusing on grammar and vocabulary. Grammar topics include articles, the passive, comparison, conditionals reporting tenses and cohesion. Vocabulary topics include prefixes and suffixes, derived nouns and adjectives, collocations and topic vocabulary related to the media. The keys to all the *Key language* exercises can be found on pages 219–220 of the Student's Book.

- The *Writing practice bank* contains ten supplementary writing exercises which fall into two groups. Guided-practice exercises are generally gapped model answers for writing tasks in the units or for additional practice tasks. Exam-task exercises provide further exam topics, but with no guidance. The keys to the guided-practice exercises of the *Writing practice bank* can be found on page 221 of the Student's Book.

1 ▶ Workout

To set the ball rolling ...

Introduce the topic briefly with books closed. For example, write up the unit title and/or the related phrasal verb *work out* (= 'do energetic exercise') as discussion points: e.g. *Does anyone here work out regularly? Why do you think joining a gym has become so popular in some countries?* It may be worth comparing this use of *work out* (intransitive) with another common meaning, 'make a calculation' (transitive).

Lead-in *(p.8)*

Check vocabulary for the activities and discuss which activities students are most/least likely to do. Invite guesses as to the correct order before revealing, or letting students check, the answer. Ask if they can draw any conclusions and point out if necessary that two very ordinary household activities, not usually thought of as 'exercise', come right in the middle of the list.

Focus on speaking 1 *Talking about personal interests (p.8)*

Read through the *Exam briefing* box, and answer any general questions students have about this aspect of the exam.

1 Invite students to ask you one or two questions first, so you can demonstrate suitably conversational answers, e.g. *Well, the thing I really hate is the exercise bike. I know it's good for me, but I just find it so boring!* If you feel your students lack fluency or confidence, practise some of the *Useful language* first. Then let them work in closed pairs to interview each other. Monitor the conversations and round off by asking a few students to report back on what their *partner* said. Doing this on a regular basis tends to encourage better listening!

2 Elicit reasons and write these on one corner of the board. They can be checked off later as students work through the text, as a way of encouraging them to think ahead about a text topic.

Focus on reading *Working out (p.9)*

1 Read through the *Exam briefing* as a class, and then give students a few minutes to study the advice. Afterwards, as reinforcement, ask them to cover the page and answer a few check questions (e.g. *What should you look at first? Why shouldn't you read the whole text carefully?*).

2 Ensure that students study the two questions before they look through the text, so they have a clear reason for reading. It may be helpful to set a time limit (say three minutes) for reading, to underline the need to skim-read rather than read intensively. Let students compare answers, and make sure everyone is absolutely clear about the correct answers and why the other options are unsuitable.

3 Again, read through the introduction with the class, and set a time limit for the task to discourage reading in depth. Check answers without discussing the paragraphs in any detail.

4/5 Ask students to read through the advice and then check briefly, e.g. *How do you know if a word is important to understand or not? What can help you guess the meaning of a word?* Let students discuss ideas about Exercise 5.

6 Read through the *Exam briefing* as a class. Summary completion is quite a demanding task, and one which needs systematic training. The worst approach is to proceed, gap by gap, through the passage, without reference to the overall context or to the original text.

Read through the introduction and *Task approach*, then give students a few moments to read through the complete gapped text and study the example, so they have a clear framework to work within.

It's a good idea to explain any unknown words in the List of Words (e.g. *vigorous, lessen*) and to run through the first two questions as a class in order to establish an effective approach.

Take them through the guidelines for Question 1 from the *Task approach* as an example, and follow the same procedure for Question 2. Ask what kind of word is missing (a word which combines with *to*, i.e. adjective or preposition). Identify examples of this type of word in the list (e.g. *according, contrary*). Find the relevant paragraph (para. 7) and check the meaning carefully (*... those who think the more intense the exercise the better are wrong*). The answer to Question 2 is *contrary*.

NB *Key language* Exercise 1 focuses on word building through the addition of the suffix *-en* (e.g. *lessen* from Exam Task 1). This is a very common way of forming verbs in English.

7 Read through the *Task approach* and focus on the definitions for Yes, No and Not Given. Make sure students are absolutely clear about the distinctions between No and Not Given answers. Double-check if necessary (*How many Yes answers are there? When do you choose Not Given?*).

Ask students to jot down the numbers of the paragraphs where relevant information for each question can be found. Check these as an interim stage (this will reinforce the *Task approach* and also help weaker students).

8 This is an important phase which can yield a lot of useful discussion. It encourages students to reflect on the task strategies they have used and to build the habit of co-operating and learning from other students. Spend time checking answers in detail, even if students have got most right. Ensure that they can justify their answers by reference to the text.

9 This exercise assumes that students are familiar with the basic parts of speech: *noun, verb, adjective,* and *adverb*. If not, it's important to introduce some basic terms now, because they represent a basic tool in preparing for IELTS and will be relevant to various tasks throughout this book. See *Key language* Exercise 2.

Students can work individually or in pairs to complete the task, but make sure they refer back to the text to study each expression in context. In feedback you could point out that words like *myth* (4), *exploded* (5) and *put off* (9) have more than one dictionary definition, and only the context will determine which is correct.

KEY LANGUAGE

- **The suffix *-en*** e.g. *less* ➔ *lessen*
  Exercise 1, page 186
  Suggested approach for classwork
  With weaker students, the exercise is best done in class, where you can clarify any adjectives which are unfamiliar, and also make sure students identify the two adjectives which require spelling changes before beginning the gap-fill task. There are a number of pairs of opposites in the list, which students could identify if time allows.
  NB There are additional *Key language* exercises on affixes (Exercise 9) which are referenced in Unit 5.
- **Grammatical terms**
  Exercise 2, page 186

Focus on vocabulary *Word partners (p.14)*

This is an introduction to collocation, the way in which some English words can be combined to form a sense unit (e.g. *winter sports*) while others can't (e.g. *snow sports*). Point out that collocation is a very important feature of English, which students need to develop an awareness of through wide reading and keeping vocabulary notebooks!

Focus on speaking 2 *Comparing and contrasting (p.15)*

1 Read through the *Exam briefing* box as a class. Ask students to suggest a few differences between the two activities before they read the practice conversation.

2 Use the first pair as an example, supplying suitable prompt words (e.g. *Both ...?, But ...? For example ...?* and eliciting appropriate comparisons. Give students time to jot down some differences between the remaining pairs, helping with ideas as necessary, then monitor their discussions.

Ask students to write up one or more comparisons as a record and to underline relevant language.

3 Again, monitor discussions and provide appropriate feedback afterwards.

Unit 1 Key

Lead-in (p.8)

See Student's Book page 216.

Focus on speaking 1 (p.8)

(*Example answers*)

2 1 It has mental and physical benefits; it keeps you
fit, helps keep weight down and also helps
prevent illnesses like heart disease.

2 Walking/swimming

Focus on reading (p.9)

2 1 c 2 d

3 1 3 2 7 3 (*example*) 4 9 5 5 6 4

5 (*Example answer*)

An illness, probably a serious one; because it's
listed with heart disease and cancer.

6	1	verb (*inf.*)	*lessen*	(para. 3: *linked with reductions in …*)
	2	adjective	*contrary*	(4: *the myth that …*)
	3	adverb	*rarely*	(6: *the most inactive people … increasing their activity;* 10: *The greatest benefits … least active do a little*)
	4	adjective	*vigorous*	(6: *high-intensity*) NB Dr Hardman does not disagree with the idea of <u>regular</u> exercise (see para. 8).
	5	verb (*sing.*)	*discourages*	(6: *All that does is put off …*)
	6	adjective	*fit*	(8: *don't just depend on how fit you are*)
	7	adjective	*active*	(8: *regular activity … use more energy*)

7	8	False	(para. 7: *She also claims … wrong*)
	9	True	(7: *Many benefits … any level of activity*)
	10	False	(9: *… the level of fat in the blood does not rise so much*) i.e. it <u>reduces</u> the rise in blood fat level. It doesn't prevent it.
	11	True	(9: *Fat and carbohydrate … are handled more quickly*)
	12	Does Not Say	(good advice but <u>not</u> mentioned in the text)
	13	False	(10: *As you increase … the risk of injury.*)

9 1 (*Example*) 6 noun (pl.); b
2 adverb; f 7 adjective; g
3 verb; i 8 verb; h
4 noun; a 9 verb; d
5 verb; e

Focus on vocabulary (p.14)

1 amateur, blood, combat, competitive, spectator,
team, water, winter

2 sports car, sports centre, sports commentator,
sports equipment, sports stadium, sportswear

Focus on speaking 2 (p.15)

2 (*Example answers*)

1 **Similarities**
- They're both good forms of exercise.
- They both take place in the water and involve
the same arm and leg movements.

Differences
- You can only swim a few metres backwards and
forwards in a swimming pool, but you can swim
as far as you like in the sea.
- Swimming in the sea is more enjoyable but you
may have to contend with waves, currents and
jellyfish. Swimming in a pool is safer but more
boring.

2 **Similarities**
- Both games involve hitting balls.
- Both can be played outside.

Differences
- Golfers use clubs and play on a golf course,
while tennis players use rackets and play on a
tennis court.
- The size of the balls and the material they're
made from are different.
- Tennis is played by two players (singles) or four
players (doubles), while golf can be played with
any number of players.
- The aim in tennis is to get the ball over the net,
while in golf the aim is to get the ball into
a hole.

3 **Similarities**
- Both involve hard, manual work, which needs
to be done regularly.
- Both usually require special equipment.

Differences
- Gardening is done in the fresh air, housework is
done indoors.
- Gardening jobs vary according to the seasons,
while housework tends to stay the same.
- Housework brings instant results, but with
gardening the results may take months or even
years to be seen.

4 **Similarities**
- Both involve energetic exercise and are done
to music.

Differences
- An aerobics class is generally for a fixed period
of time, while a party can last all night.
- People usually eat and drink at a party, as well
as dancing.
- With aerobics, there is a teacher who decides
what steps or movements should be done and
for how long, but at a party people are free to
decide exactly what they do.

2 ▶ Food for thought

To set the ball rolling ...

Introduce the topic briefly, with books closed. You could discuss typical breakfasts in different countries, the more varied the better, e.g. 'full English breakfast' (fried egg, bacon, sausage, tomato and fried bread) or Japanese *natto* (fermented soya beans). Ask how healthy these are and why. It's important not to express judgement at this stage, to avoid pre-empting later discussions. If time allows, you could also discuss students' own preferred breakfasts.

Lead-in *(p.16)*

Using the introductory question *Who eats more healthily: men or women?*, ask students to vote for either men or women, and keep a note of the result.

1 Once students have looked through the table, check any unfamiliar vocabulary, e.g. *fibre, cereal, wholemeal (bread)*. You could help by telling them there are five healthy and five unhealthy habits. Make sure they discuss ideas with their partner, rather than working alone. Ask a few pairs to report on their decisions and reasons, before they check the answers.

2 Focus on the 'Why?' part of the question, encouraging students to formulate a satisfactory answer. If necessary, prompt them with: *Women tend to eat more … and consume less … .* Point out the usefulness of qualifying expressions like *generally* and *tend to*.

Focus on speaking *Eating habits (p.16)*

These are typical of questions that might be asked in Part 1 of the Speaking Test. Point out that answers should be as full as possible and monitor students' discussions carefully, giving appropriate feedback afterwards.

Focus on writing 1 *Interpreting information from diagrams (p.17)*

NB Since decisions about tenses are relevant in most writing tasks, it's important that students can name at least the main tenses. If they are at all hazy in this area, refer them to the reference list of tenses (*Key language, Exercise 3, page 187*). You may also wish to go through the accompanying exercise in class or set it for homework.

Read through the *Exam briefing* as a class and discuss any questions students have.

1 Give students time to read the paragraphs and study the graphs, and then let them compare answers and ideas. After checking their answers, ask what they think the two vertical scales represent (A: grams per person per week; B: percentages). Then read through the two paragraphs again, highlighting each key expression. Focus on the word *trend* and point out that identifying overall trends is one of the most important aspects of graph interpretation.

2 Read through the expressions in the box, checking understanding as necessary, before students do the task.

3 Monitor students' work and, after checking, focus on the organisation of the text, looking at how different components of the graph are linked (coherence).

If they are having problems, give extra practice with these or other graphs before doing Exercise 4. This could be in the form of *Give me a sentence about the graph using 'reached a peak'*, for example.

4 This is suitable for class or homework.

NB There is a short *Key language* exercise on reporting tenses, which could be done in class or for homework.

KEY LANGUAGE
• **Names of tenses**   Exercise 3, page 187   • **Reporting tenses**   Exercise 4, page 188

Focus on listening 1 *Students' Union survey (p.19)*

Students may be alarmed at the idea of only hearing the recording once in the exam; training needs to strike a balance between developing listening skills and confidence, and accustoming students to the once-only format. For the first few tasks, you could play the recording again on request. Later on, you could read out problematic sections of the recording script for clarification and as a support to weaker students.

NB The recording is in two sections and, unless your students are very able, you may prefer to prepare for, and possibly check, each section separately.

Read through the *Exam briefing* and give students a few minutes to study the instructions and Questions 1 to 7. It's also a good idea to ask a few check questions, e.g. *What's the survey about? How do you mark the correct answer? Are all the questions of the same type? How many words can you use to answer the last three questions?* You could also let them discuss the food illustrated in Questions 2 and 3.

Allow time for comparing answers before the checking phase. Afterwards, you could focus on a few useful or interesting expressions, e.g. *I've never been (that) keen on ..., once in a blue moon, to skip (breakfast), to have a sweet tooth.*

NB If students have difficulties with the spelling in Question 8, it's worth giving further practice (e.g. British or Australian place names: Leicester, Swansea, Bathurst, Kalgoorlie), since this is a fairly regular feature of the exam.

Focus on listening 2 *Healthy eating (p.20)*

Allow plenty of time for the pre-listening phase. It's important that students guess answers in advance because, apart from encouraging the prediction strategy, by checking their answers when they listen, they will be practising the skills for a slightly different note-completion task. (There is an example in Unit 4.)

Read through the *Exam briefing* section and instructions.

Before students work together to guess answers, you could look at the first two questions to focus on the kind of word or expression required (Question 1: adjective modifying noun, e.g. *good, healthy*; Question 2: either a general adverb like *much* or a more specific comparison like *three times*). Emphasise that it is the thinking which is important, not guessing the right answer. Even making a wild guess will make the listening process easier.

Before playing the recording, check that students have filled in all the spaces in pencil. You could also check a few predictions, especially for Question 9, and deal with any unknown vocabulary (e.g. *poultry*).

As a possible follow-up, you might want to focus on the difference between the two comparisons heard: *twice/three times as much* versus *ten/twenty times more.*

Focus on writing 2 *Paragraphing (p.21)*

Remind students of the information in the *Exam briefing* (Student's Book page 17) if necessary.

1 Inappropriate paragraphing, or a failure to paragraph at all, remains a common weakness in IELTS written work for Task 2. This introductory task is intended to underline the importance of paragraphing in communicating clearly to the reader. Discussions should cover both when to begin a new paragraph (with each main new idea) and how to do this clearly (indent or miss a line). Point out, if necessary, that

paragraphing is highly relevant to Task 2 of the Writing module, but that it may be unnecessary to divide Task 1 answers into paragraphs when they are shorter and deal with a single topic.

2 Cohesion is a major factor in good writing, and this topic will recur later in the book. Ask students to study the two paragraphs and elicit ideas. In discussion, introduce the terms **grammatical link** (e.g. *which*) and **logical link** (e.g. *but*). Then let them look through the reference list(s) in detail. You could point out that there is a fuller list of reference links in the *Key language bank* (page 193), but it's probably best to leave the exercises there till a later stage.

3/4/5 Give students time to work on the tasks alone and then compare answers. There are, of course, several acceptable ways of rewriting the text in Exercise 5.

Spot the error *(p.22)*

This is a good task for students to work on in pairs. Make sure they check answers by reference to the *Error Hit List*, and encourage them to add extra errors from their own written work for this unit. Check that the corrections are accurate!

Unit 2 Key

Lead-in (p.16)

1 See Student's Book page 216.

2 Women generally have healthier diets than men because they tend to eat more fruit and vegetables on a daily basis, and they consume less sugar and fat.

Focus on writing 1 (p.17)

1

Graph	Paragraph	Activity
A	2	meat consumption
B	1	cigarette smoking

2 b 1 a slight/marginal rise (in)
   2 between 2000 and 2003; during the period 2000 to 2003
   3 a sharp decrease/fall (in)
   4 to increase rapidly
   5 to be at/reach a peak
   6 to level out
3 1 a significant decline 2 (corresponding) rise
   3 reached a peak 4 a steady/marked decline/fall
   5 exceeded 6 a marked fall/decline
   7 in about 1984 8 a steady/significant increase/rise
   9 1994
4 (*Example answers*)
There was a gradual decline in the sales of **LPs** from 1978 until about 1988. After that, sales fell more steeply until 1993, and then remained at a very low level.
Sales of **cassettes** rose steadily for a period of about fifteen years from 1973. Having reached a peak of about 90 million in 1989, sales began to decline, and by 1997, they had fallen to about 40 million.
There was a rapid increase in the sale of **CDs** after their introduction in 1983, and by about 1991, sales exceeded those of LPs. They continued to rise steeply for the next few years, reaching a peak of about 160 million in 1996.

Focus on listening 1 (p.19)

1 B 2 C 3 B 4 C 5 C 6 B 7 A
8 Buckingham 9 Travel and Tourism
10 Second/2nd

Focus on listening 2 (p.20)

1 balanced 2 twenty (20) times 3 five (5)
4 carbonated 5 dairy products
6 three or four (3/4) 7 salt 8 three times a/per
9 avocado (pear) 10 twice as much

Focus on writing 2 (p.21)

1 a New paragraphs should begin at:
The reason people put on weight …
Surveys show that …
1 b 1 When writing about a subject where there are several aspects to be considered, for example an argument, a report or a detailed description; to enable the writer to organise his/her ideas clearly and to make it easier for the reader to follow them.
   2 When you want to introduce a main new idea or topic.
2 Paragraph A is unnecessarily repetitive, and it is not clear which of the three sentences contains the main idea. By comparison, in paragraph B the three sentences have been linked together grammatically (*which*) and logically (*but*), making it easy to identify the main idea.
3 A although; Moreover
   B Because; To; When
4 C (Before) that; such (societies); These (communities); those (prevailing); They
   D the (meat eaten); that (found); which
5 (*Example answers*)
   A We know that pizzas were eaten in ancient Pompeii, <u>since</u> brick pizza ovens have been uncovered <u>there</u> by archaeologists. <u>However</u>, early pizzas would have lacked one of their main modern ingredients <u>because</u> the first tomato seeds were not brought to Europe from Peru until 1,500 years later.
   B <u>Although</u> tomatoes were held in low esteem by most Europeans, the poor people of Naples added <u>them</u> to their yeast dough <u>and</u> created the first modern pizza. By the 17th century, pizza was popular with visitors, <u>who</u> would go to poor neighbourhoods to taste <u>the</u> peasant dish, <u>(which was)</u> made by men called *pizzaioli*.

Spot the error (p.22)

1 (*Example*)
2 There <u>was a gradual increase in</u> smoking.
3 … an increase <u>in</u> expenditure …
4 <u>Consumption of butter</u> has fallen sharply … / <u>There has been a fall in the consumption</u> of …
5 <u>Sales of</u> margarine <u>have</u> also fallen …
6 The popularity of CDs has <u>increased</u> … / CDs <u>have increased in popularity</u> …
7 There was a fall <u>in</u> the rate of inflation …
8 The standard of living … has <u>risen</u>.

3 ▶ Location is everything

To set the ball rolling ...

Ask students to name the odd one out from a list of cities on the board, e.g. *Paris, New York, Bangkok, Cairo, London, Buenos Aires* (odd one out = New York – not a capital city). Follow up with a few general questions, e.g. *Have you visited any of these cities? Which city would you most like to visit? Is it better to live in a city than in the country? Why/Why not?*

Lead-in *(p.24)*

1 This is a short activity for pair discussion, which touches on some of the topics in the reading passage. Students can check the answers on page 216, but you may prefer to supply them yourself. NB If students are interested and you have time to discuss them, the Key contains some additional facts and figures.

2 Let students read through the descriptions individually and then discuss ideas in pairs. If they need help, tell them they can choose from the list of cities on page 24, and if they are still struggling, you could supply the following extra clues:

> **A** It was a British Crown Colony until 1997.
> **B** The Olympic Games were held there in 2000.
> **C** One of its suburbs is associated with the film industry.
> **D** Bicycles are a common form of transport in the city centre.

Ask students to say how they identified the cities and use the checking phase to highlight any interesting/useful expressions, e.g. **A** *container (port)* **B** *mistakenly* (<u>think</u>/<u>believe</u>) **C** *land area <u>devoted</u> to roads* **D** *the seat of government, the stock exchange*

Afterwards, students could create their own city descriptions for others to guess, if time allows.

NB *Key language* Exercise 5 revises the form and use of the passive voice. This exercise could be included at this early stage to highlight the importance of the passive in academic writing.

KEY LANGUAGE

- **The passive**
  Exercise 5, page 188
  Suggested approach for classwork
- Write the example active sentence on the board and check that students can identify the *subject* and *object*. Elicit the passive version and write it up.
- Check the term *agent*, and introduce the terms *long* and *short passive*. Ask which is more common, and what kind of writing they would expect to find most examples of the short passive in. Students can check answers in the *Language fact* box (page 189).
- If you feel your students would benefit from a more detailed analysis of the form, you could look at the various tenses possible and also the use of the infinitive, with and without *to* (e.g. *He asked to be excused. The problem could be solved.*)

Focus on speaking 1 *Urban problems (p.25)*

1/2 It's worth pointing out that urban problems, such as population growth, are a very common IELTS topic. Let students check answers to Exercise 2 before they move on to the next exercise.

3 If mindmapping is new to students, it's best to work through the initial stages as a class. Ask students to suggest more headings (e.g. Population, Pollution), and to add examples. It's important not to be too prescriptive, nor to complete the task at this stage. Point out that there isn't one 'right answer', and that each mindmap will reflect an individual way of thinking.

Focus on reading *Location is everything (p.26)*

1 Ask students to cover the text before eliciting answers to Exercise 1a. Then give them a minute or so to skim the text. Check answers carefully to make sure they have a real overview (i.e. an idea of the <u>whole</u> text, rather than any one aspect of it).

2 Let students compare ideas before checking answers.

3 Read through the *Exam briefing* and *Task approach*. Encourage students to write on the reading text and point out that they can and should write on the exam paper, which may surprise them.

Ask students to highlight the cities **A–I** in the text. (Make sure they don't include other place names.) The text doesn't always specify which country a city is in, and although it's not strictly necessary to know this, being able to 'place' a city is probably helpful in terms of confidence. So, if your students' general knowledge is shaky, you may want to check that they know where one or two cities are, and also the modern name for Constantinople (Istanbul).

Focus on the example and ask students to find the relevant parallel expressions in the text (grew into a successful trading city = *was prospering thanks to trade*; location close to the sea = *proximity to the sea*). It may be helpful to repeat this procedure for the first question, as a class.

Let students compare answers, and when checking, make sure they can justify their answers by reference to the text. You may need to clarify one or two vocabulary items, e.g. *swamp* (Question 4) and *periphery* (Question 6).

4/5/6 Sentence completion is quite a challenging task-type, and this introduction will probably need to be paced quite slowly, with time to complete the introductory tasks, and plenty of support in tackling the task itself.

Read through the *Task approach* and then ask students to complete Exercises 5 and 6 and compare answers before checking.

7 Read through the instructions and example. It would help to do Question 9 as a class. Ask students to think of another word for *farming* and elicit *agriculture*. Tell them to find where this word first appears (line 7) and read the information carefully, before choosing the best ending. Check that they can justify the answer (I) *live permanently in one place = settle down and live …*

It's important that students use their reading skills rather than their guessing skills to complete the task! Monitor to make sure they are reading the text carefully.

Let students compare answers and check they can identify the relevant parallel phrases in the text.

Focus on speaking 2 *Describing places (p.30)*

If your students are on a shorter, intensive course, you may want to remind them of the format of the interview and also clarify what is expected in Part 2. Emphasise how important it is to keep talking. When the task is a description, it's especially important to think of several aspects of the subject to talk about. Point out that mindmaps are a useful way of making brief notes.

1 Monitor the pairwork and ask one or two students to report back on what their partner said.

2 Make sure students realise they have to refer to the maps to complete the text. Afterwards, check vocabulary as necessary, e.g. *in the west* versus **to the west**; *attractions* versus *amenities*.

3 Where there are two (or more) students of the same nationality, they can usefully work together in pairs or small groups to make notes. However, students should swap groups/pairs before giving their descriptions. Monitor carefully, noting key areas for attention. For additional speaking practice, students could use the same headings to compare their own cities, or to compare their city with the place they will be studying at (ask the question *What differences do you expect?*).

NB There is a *Key language* exercise on describing geographical positions (see below). This should be a fairly quick revision, but it's an important area and there are some points which are well worth clarifying.

KEY LANGUAGE

- **Geographical positions**
  Exercise 6, page 189
  Suggested approach for classwork
- Let students work in pairs to read and discuss Questions 1–4. When checking, add further examples to clarify, as necessary.
- For Question 5, students should work individually before checking answers in pairs. With weaker students, it may be worth getting them to write out their answers, and checking their use of capitals carefully.
- Use the other places marked for extra oral or written practice as necessary.

Spot the error *(p.31)*

This is a good task for pairwork. Make sure students do the exercise before referring to the *Error Hit List*. Check that corrections are accurate, and encourage students to add extra errors from their own written work for this unit.

Unit 3 Key

Lead-in (p.24)

1 NB These answers are given in the Student's Book, but more detail is included here.

1 Tokyo (27.2 million)

2 Rome (c. one million)

3 Bombay (annual growth rate: 4.22%)

4 Mexico City (2,255m above sea level)

5 London (opened 1863, compared with Paris 1900, New York 1904, Tokyo 1927). London also has the longest underground network, with 400km of track, although New York's has more stations. The busiest underground railway is in Moscow.

6 Chicago (66.4 million passengers per year, compared with London Heathrow 44.2 million, Frankfurt 27.5 million and Paris Charles de Gaulle 25.6 million)

2 NB These answers are also given in the Student's Book, but more detail is included here.

A Hong Kong, China (population density: 5,858 people per square kilometre)

B Sydney, Australia (the capital is Canberra)

C Los Angeles, USA (the centre of the film industry is, of course, Hollywood)

D Amsterdam, Netherlands (the official seat of government is The Hague)

Focus on speaking 1 (p.25)

1 (environmental) pollution

1 The large number of cars and also the geographical situation of Los Angeles, surrounded by hills.

2 (*Example answer*)

Because pollution can cause serious health problems.

3 (*Example answers*)

Fuel could be taxed more heavily; public transport could be improved; alternative 'greener' forms of fuel should be developed.

2 See Student's Book page 216.

3 (*Example answers*)

Crime: e.g. drug-related crime, young offenders, growing prison population

Population: e.g. migration to cities, population explosion

Employment: e.g. lack of employment opportunities

Transport: e.g. traffic congestion, pollution

Housing/Living conditions: homelessness, slum housing, lack of basic services (gas/electricity/water)

Healthcare: e.g. need for sufficient trained doctors/ nurses, hospital equipment, drugs

Education: e.g. need for sufficient trained teachers, books, school equipment

Other: e.g. care of the elderly, environmental awareness

Focus on reading (p.26)

1 a (*Example answer*)

The importance of location in the development of the world's major cities.

2 2

3 1 D *banking came to dominate its economy* (lines 68–69)

2 F *By the 1930s ... New York ... world's first city with a population of ten million* (112–117)

3 A *became rich by weaving wool* (66)

4 B *founded ... on swamp land* (91)

5 C *largest city and premiere trading centre* (71–72)

6 E *stations are dotted around the periphery* (instead of located centrally) (107–108)

7 G *the city's power went into steep decline* (33–34)

8 H *Thousands of slave labourers died during its construction* (99–100)

5 1 citizens, inhabitants   **2** depended on, couldn't manage without   **3** followed, came afterwards   **4** leaving, abandoning   **5** migrating back, returning   **6** started developing, appeared   **7** easy to reach, convenient to get to   **8** ridiculously, foolishly   **9** huge, enormous

6 1 9, 11, 13   **2** 10, 12, 14

7 *Example*: not so many = *fewer*; were required = *were needed*

9 I   farming = *agriculture*; live permanently in one place (I) = *settle down and live*

10 C   protection = *defensive*

11 G   began to grow and prosper = *flourished*; made money (G) = *became wealthier*

12 D   lost its power = *went into steep decline*; its dependence on (D) = *became reliant on*

13 A   established = *founded*; convenient (A) = *accessible*

14 E   religious (E) = *sacred*

Focus on speaking 2 (p.30)

2 1 (situated) in the west   **2** population   **3** is (situated) on / lies on   **4** includes   **5** called   **6** in/near the   **7** (to the) north-west   **8** (tourist) attractions   **9** amenities

Spot the error (p.31)

1 ... a large/considerable/substantial amount ...

2 A number of cities have ...

3 ✓

4 ... have a high level ...

5 A number of surveys have been ...

6 Only a small percentage of the houses have ...

7 ✓

8 ... a higher standard of living.

9 ... is not in proportion to the size...

10 Compared with ...

4 ▶ Haves and have-nots

TO SET THE BALL ROLLING ...

As this unit develops a topic area related to Unit 3, there is no need for a separate introduction. However, you could take a few minutes to revise useful topic vocabulary from the previous unit, e.g. *megacity, accessible, amenities,* together with language points from *Spot the error* and/or the *Key language.*

Lead-in *(p.32)*

1 This brief introduction is an opportunity to highlight some topic areas and to check some key topic vocabulary.

2 Ensure students work in pairs. Although they're unlikely to know the answers, encourage them to discuss the questions and make intelligent guesses. Make sure they have marked their chosen answers before checking.
NB The Key on page 17 includes some interesting comparative figures which are not in the Student's Book.

Focus on writing 1 *Interpreting and comparing data (p.33)*

1 As an alternative to the procedure in the book, and for speed, you could read out the questions, inviting students to guess answers (without accepting or rejecting these). Move on quickly to the following task without letting students check answers!

2 This orientation task needs to be completed quickly if it's to develop key skimming/scanning skills, so set a tight time limit (say one minute). When checking answers, ask for key words from the diagrams (e.g. C *read and write* = literacy). Make sure students label the diagrams correctly before continuing.

3/4 Let students collaborate on these tasks if they want, and again set a time limit. Briefly check answers to Exercise 4 in relation to previous guesses.

5 Monitor students' work and use this exercise for diagnostic purposes.

NB If you detect a general weakness in this area of comparatives, do *Key language* Exercise 7 (see below) as a class, <u>before</u> moving on to Exercise 6. Otherwise, set it for individual or class homework.

6 There is more scope for error here, so monitor carefully in order to steer weaker students in the right direction.

7 The information in the table is quite complex, in that units of measurement vary and high figures may be good (e.g. clean air) or bad (e.g. murders). For this reason, it's worth spending time making sure that students are absolutely clear about the correct interpretations.

As an introduction, you could ask a few preliminary questions, e.g. (Los Angeles): *What does the figure 12.5 represent? And 12.4? Is that high or low?* (Noise): *Which is quietest: 1 or 10?* (NB *ambient* means 'in the surrounding area'.) Students might find it helpful to circle the best or worst figures in each area with different colours prior to discussion.

Include the writing phase in class time if possible, so that students can exchange ideas and you can monitor their work.

NB If your students need extra support, you could design a gap-fill exercise based on the suggested answers in the Key. Monitor students' work and use this task as a diagnostic tool to help you decide whether to do *Key language* Exercise 8 on comparatives (see below) as a class, or recommend it to individuals.

KEY LANGUAGE

- **Numerical and other comparative expressions**
  Exercise 7, page 190
- **Forming comparatives and superlatives**
  Exercise 8, page 191

Focus on listening 1 *Wasting energy (p.35)*

NB The recording is in two sections, and unless your students are very able, you may prefer to prepare for, and possibly check, each section separately.

In this case, read through the *Exam briefing* and give students a few minutes to look at the *Task approach,* and study the bar graph for Questions 1 and 2.

At the end of the first section, pause the recording. (You could also check answers at this stage.) Give students time to read through Questions 3–10 and invite some guesses as to possible answers.

After playing the recording, give students time to compare their answers. If necessary, replay the recording, section by section, as you check answers.

Focus on writing 2 *Paragraphing* (p.37)

Inappropriate paragraphing in exam written work can be as much of a problem as not paragraphing, and students need to be aware that paragraphs rarely consist of a single sentence. Before you begin, briefly revise the reasons for paragraphing discussed in Unit 2.

1/2/3/4 Check that students are quite clear about the terms *topic*, *supporting* and *qualifying*, and clarify further if necessary. Make sure there's an agreed order for the sentences in Exercise 3 before they go on to Exercise 4. Remind them of the linking expressions in Unit 2, and refer them back to the lists on pages 21 and 22 if necessary, before they begin.

5 Read through the *Exam briefing* as a class and then let students study the exam topic. Point out that mindmaps are a very useful way of organising your thoughts in preparation for writing (as well as speaking), and ask them to find the mindmap they drew up in Unit 3 (page 26).

Ask students to work in pairs to:

1 add new headings/ideas from the information in this unit (e.g. Employment and Education);

2 decide which two problems are the most important or urgent to tackle;

3 discuss possible strategies for tackling them.

Have a round-up of ideas before continuing (or combine pairs to swap ideas). The writing task could usefully be done in class if time allows, so that students can benefit from some immediate feedback. Otherwise, set it for homework.

Focus on listening 2 *Case study: São Paulo (p.38)*

NB Again, you may prefer to prepare for each section of the recording separately.

Before playing the first section, you could also ask students to suggest a few facts they know about Brazil. Then let them look through the instructions and Questions 1–4, and discuss which answers they think are correct. Remind them that they must follow the lecture and answer questions *while* they listen.

At the end of the first section, pause the recording. (You may wish to check answers at this stage.) Give students time to refer to the *Task approach* for completing diagrams (page 35), or revise orally if you prefer. Focus their attention on the layout: **main heading** (centre) and **subheadings** (around), and also ask them to check which way the questions go: clockwise or anticlockwise.

Give students time to study the instructions and Questions 5–10. Point out that, in the exam, they can write more than three words in the question booklet if necessary and then transfer the three key words to the answer sheet.

Let students compare answers before checking. You may want to replay the recording as you check answers, to clear up any misunderstandings, and also focus on useful expressions such as *shanty towns, settle in, stumbling block.*

Unit 4 Key

Lead-in *(p.32)*

1 (*Example answers and notes*)
1 The very rapid (*exponential*) rate of increase in recent years.
2 Clean water, living conditions (housing, sanitation, etc.), hygiene, diet, healthcare, immunisation + genes.
3 Life expectancy, literacy, school enrolment and educational attainment (the criteria used by the UN's *Human Development Index* in analysing quality of life, in addition to per capita GDP). Other possible factors might include: air quality, crime figures, health and educational facilities, as well as more contentious issues like the position of women and freedom of expression.

2 See Student's Book page 216.

Additional notes
6 The criteria for calculating rankings are the ones listed for Question 3 in Exercise 1 of the *Lead-in*. The full top ten is as follows:
  1 Norway   5 Belgium   9 Japan
  2 Australia   6 United States 10 Finland
  3 Canada   7 Iceland
  4 Sweden   8 Netherlands
7 The other top-five countries were:
  2 UK (86.6%)
  3 Germany (86.4%)
  4 Canada (84.9%)
  5 France (74.3%)
  (Source: National Center for Education Statistics, US Department of Education, 1999)
10 The world average is 22 per 1,000. (Source: *The World Factbook* 2000)

Focus on writing 1 *(p.33)*

1 1 an Australian   2 Europe   3 Latvia   4 country
5 city
2 1 B   2 C   3 D   4 A

3 1 numbers of years
2 women; in Australia
3 five; countries
4 numbers of patients per doctor
5 Latvia
6 literacy levels in different continents
7 Female, Male
8 percentages (of the population)
9 77% (52% + 25%)
10 83% (37% + 46%)

5 A 1 identical   2 twice   3 the greatest
B 4 twenty times
C 5 much lower   6 (very) little (NB *a marginal* is also possible)
D 7 (exactly) a quarter   8 almost half

6 (*Example answers*)
1 Africa is the continent with the greatest difference in literacy rates between men and women. / In Africa the literacy rate for men is almost 50% **higher than** that for women.
2 Doctors in Nepal have 100/one hundred times **as many** patients **as** doctors in Latvia. / Doctors in Nepal have 100/one hundred times **more** patients **than** …
3 In 1990, 58% of the world's population lived in rural areas, but by 2025, this is expected to be **much lower**.

7 a 1 London   **2** Mexico City   **3** Mexico City
4 Tokyo   **5** Los Angeles   **6** London and Tokyo
c (*Example answers*)
1 With a population of 13.6 million, Shanghai is only slightly larger than Los Angeles and it also has similar figures for noise levels, the provision of basic services and the percentage of children in secondary school. However, on two very important counts, Shanghai scores higher than LA. In the first place, it is a very much safer city to live in, with a murder rate which is only one fifth that of LA. In addition, the air quality is much better, so it is a healthier city to live in. The only disadvantage, according to the figures, would be that there is a higher level of traffic congestion in Shanghai in the rush hour.
2 Of the five cities, Tokyo appears to have the best environment overall. Although it is by far the largest of the five, with a population of 27.2 million, it is also the safest city to live in, with a murder rate of only 1.4 per 100,000. In addition, it has the least traffic congestion, the lowest levels of ambient noise and the highest percentage of children in secondary school. The provision of basic services is excellent, and the quality of its air is relatively good.

Focus on listening 1 (*p.35*)
1 Tokyo   2 Calcutta   3 twenty (20) days   4 damp
5 80   6 Plastics   7 4,000 years   8 temperature
9 humidity   10 oxygen

Focus on writing 2 (*p.37*)
1 a The influence of the car on the design of modern cities.
b The first sentence = the topic statement. Supporting points = 1 high level of car ownership reflected in low-density layout of cities; 2 freeway systems designed to facilitate regular long-distance driving.
2 The last sentence.
3 Topic statement 3
Supporting point(s) 1
Qualifying statement 5
Supporting point(s) 2, 4
4 (*Example answer*)
In the past, waste disposal was cheap and easy, <u>as</u> much rubbish was simply dumped in a convenient place. Today, <u>however</u>, there are numerous problems, <u>including</u> increased transport costs, <u>which</u> make waste disposal expensive, <u>and</u> a shortage of suitable space for depositing waste.

Focus on listening 2 (*p.38*)
1 16.5 million
2 ✓
3 cars and computers
4 ✓
5 not enough/lack of money
6 Floods
7 variety of work
8 entertainment
9 (hospitals and) health
10 transport

5 ▶ Hurry sickness

TO SET THE BALL ROLLING ...

Minimal introduction is needed, but a picture (or demonstration) of an untidy desk might be a useful springboard. Ask if it looks familiar, or how it makes students feel, and discuss briefly who considers themselves organised/disorganised, and whether tidiness is important. (You could mention that, according to a study carried out by the British Association for the Advancement of Science, an untidy desk can actually be the sign of a sophisticated mind!)

Lead-in (p.40)

With weaker students, you may need to provide vocabulary input. You could also vary the teaching order slightly by dealing with vocabulary (Exercise 2a) immediately after Question 1 of Exercise 1, before returning to the two discussion questions.

NB *Prioritise* and *clutter* feature in *Focus on listening* 2 in Unit 6.

Focus on speaking *Personal priorities (p.41)*

As an alternative approach, students could work in pairs to try and reach agreement on their lists. Either way, monitor pairwork to ensure that the topics are being discussed in reasonable depth and also to note any language areas which need attention. Finish with a round-up of opinions and feedback, as necessary.

NB These are suitable issues for Task 2 writing topics, too.

Focus on reading 1 *Hurry sickness (p.41)*

1 a Help students explore ideas about the title: Is it a real illness? How does *hurry* relate to the idea of modern life? How is life different today from 100 years ago? etc. You could mention that 'hurry sickness' is also known as 'acceleration disorder' and 'compression tiredness'.

 b Set a time limit of four to five minutes for global reading (skimming) to prevent students getting bogged down by reading this quite dense text in detail. When checking, look also at why wrong answers are wrong and emphasise, as ever, the need to have a clear idea of the overall topic.

2 Introduce the term 'scanning' if necessary, and point out that being able to locate specific information in a long reading passage quickly is an essential skill for many exam questions.

3 Read through the introduction and *Task approach*, and then work through the initial steps, as a class. Ask students to cover the list of headings and give them time to read through Section A briskly – not in exhaustive detail. Compare ideas for summaries before checking the correct answer. Repeat for Section D. Ask if these headings summarise or pick out key information.

 The exam task itself is intended to be fairly straightforward and confidence-building. When checking, ask students to justify their answers by reference to the text.

4/5 While students should be familiar with conventional multiple-choice questions (Question 7), they may not have met the variation shown in Questions 8–11, which is a common IELTS task-type. Read through the *Task approach*, paying special attention to the three key questions. Point out that in questions like 8–11, answers can be given in any order, and stress the need to find evidence for the correct answers in the text.

6 Since this differs from the previous example in Unit 1, make sure students notice the key instruction: that answers must be words or phrases from the text. Remind them of the importance of scanning to find the relevant section before reading for detail. If students are struggling, you can help by giving them paragraph references, e.g. Question 12 (paragraph B), Question 13 (paragraph C), etc.

7 This exercise encourages self-help skills in dealing with vocabulary in reading texts. Before beginning, remind students about the guidelines for dealing with unknown vocabulary (page 10). While checking, clarify further as necessary.

NB Affixes are also a useful clue to working out the meaning of words, and there are *Key language* exercises in this area of language (see below). If some or all of your students would benefit from practice in this area of language, these exercises can be completed in class or set for homework.

KEY LANGUAGE

- **Affixes**
  Exercise 9, page 192
  Suggested approach for classwork
- Introduce the terms *affix, prefix* and *suffix* with examples on the board and then let students work through the three tasks.
- Further concept checking and/or clarification may be necessary, especially with Task 3 (The prefix *over-*), where there may be confusion between certain items, e.g. *overrun* vs *be overdue*.
- Set a task requiring students to use this vocabulary.

Focus on reading 2
Distinguishing fact from opinion (p.47)

This is a brief introduction to an important reading skill, which is required for a range of IELTS reading questions. The aim is to raise students' awareness of the kind of verbal clues which suggest that the writer is expressing a subjective opinion. Let students compare answers and discuss as necessary.

Unit 5 Key

Lead-in *(p.40)*
2a **1** to prioritize (US spelling; UK spelling is *prioritise*) **2** down-to-earth **3** clutter **4** to delegate **5** peak

Focus on reading 1 *(p.41)*
1b C
2 **1** stress-related illnesses **2** nearly 40 years **3** sociology
3 **1** vii **2** ix **3** iii **4** vi **5** x **6** ii
4 **7** B *people pull their cell phones out …* (section D)
8–11 (in any order)
B *human beings are not designed …* (section E)
D *there is increased pressure to do more …* (C)
E *In the past, an overnight letter …* (C)
H *Because the technology is available to us, …* (C)
5 • Results of hurry sickness rather than causes: C, F
• Factors not mentioned in the text: A, G
6 **12** degree and intensity (B) **13** technology (C) **14** (physical) health (E) **15** symptoms/ disorders (F) / (serious) health problems (E) **16** become aware of (H)
7 **1** I **2** E **3** H **4** J **5** A **6** C **7** F **8** G **9** B **10** D

Focus on reading 2 *(p.47)*
1 **1** On my way to work once, … razor (F); which seemed to me extraordinary. (O)
2 James Gleick is a science writer and the author of several books … (F) … fascinating … (O)
3 F
4 … the undoubted speed of the Internet (F), there's a sense … impatient (O)
2 **1** O **6** F
2 F **7** O
3 O **8** O
4 F **9** O
5 O **10** F

6 ▶ Time out

TO SET THE BALL ROLLING ...

Ask students to guess which leisure activities are most popular in the UK. (Walking is by far the most popular physical activity/sport, while watching TV is the most popular home-based activity.) You could also mention that DIY, gardening and driving for pleasure are top-ten pastimes. Then briefly discuss this in relation to popular leisure activities in students' countries.

Lead-in *(p.48)*

1 Check that students are ticking boxes in the correct column. Before the pair discussion, you could demonstrate the wide variety of questions that can be asked by quizzing one or two students about one of their chosen activities. Monitor students' conversations and note any errors to deal with, as necessary.

2 NB Students should think about the different age groups in relation to a specific country, probably the one where you are teaching.

  a Check instructions beforehand and have a brief round-up of ideas afterwards.

  b This discussion can be in pairs or as a class.

NB The table of results on page 207 provides a good basis for oral and guided written practice in comparing data (see *Writing practice* Exercise 1 below).

WRITING PRACTICE

- **Presenting and comparing data (guided practice)** Exercise 1, page 207
  Suggested approach for classwork
- **Oral practice:** This works particularly well if you have an OHP and can prepare a transparency of the table. Ask students to identify the most interesting four or five differences in the figures and to describe them, e.g. *Twice as many people in the 25–29 age group do DIY as 16–19-year-olds.*
- **Written practice:** This exercise can be completed in class or set for homework. There is also an opportunity to focus on linking expressions such as *For example, On the other hand, However,* together with the opening and closing sentences.

Focus on vocabulary *Describing people (p.49)*

1 This activity is best done with books closed so that students are not distracted by the lists of adjectives. Check understanding of the activities if necessary (a

kayak is a kind of canoe, in which the place where you sit is covered over).

2 Students can work alone or in pairs. Explain any unknown vocabulary (e.g. *cerebral, introspective*). When checking, ask them to single out the attributes which helped them identify each activity.

3 This activity can be done in pairs, or for speed, as a class. Clarify vocabulary in the Key on page 216 as necessary (e.g. *carefree, outdoor type*).

Optional activity: Ask students to write four to five adjectives on a piece of paper to describe someone who enjoys <u>their</u> favourite activity. Collect students' lists (with names for identification) and read out a few to the class to see if the activities can be guessed.

4 This activity is useful practice for Part 2 of the Speaking paper. Make sure students make notes beforehand (preferably using mindmaps) and monitor their discussions, noting areas for improvement.

Focus on listening 1 *Student interviews (p.50)*

Allow time for pairwork preparation and check ideas quickly. After playing the recording, let students compare answers before checking and, if time allows, focus on interesting expressions, e.g. *swings and roundabouts* (a situation where the disadvantages are balanced by the advantages), *they <u>take your mind off</u> your work; the equipment's <u>out of the Ark</u>* (very old or old-fashioned).

Focus on speaking *Leisure activities (p.50)*

Read through the *Exam briefing* as a class.

1 Point out that there are always two main elements to a Part 2 topic – **describe** and **explain** – and that you need to do both well in order to get good marks.

2 Discuss students' ideas, and see if they can think of any additional headings which might be relevant for other activities (e.g. Costs, Training).

3 Encourage them to think of appropriate headings for their activity rather than using the ones in the example. Monitor the note-making, helping as necessary.

4 Monitor the conversations while keeping an eye on the time.

5 Monitor discussions and afterwards give feedback and vocabulary input, as appropriate.

Focus on listening 2 *Ten ways to slow down your life (p.51)*

Begin by asking what kind of things cause stress in life, and inviting suggestions for ways of dealing with it. As students study the questions, ask them to underline 'signpost' words which help identify the kind of word needed, e.g. *a/the, and, avoid*.

After checking answers, you could focus on interesting expressions, e.g. *workload, to skip, to talk shop, to give (something) a miss. Prioritise* and *clutter* figured in the Lead-in to Unit 5.

Focus on writing *Structuring an argument (p.52)*

1/2 Read through the *Task approach* as a class. Once students have read through the question, have a brief class discussion on the topic to gauge initial reactions. Then let students talk about the points and invite brief feedback.

3/4 Students should work in pairs to discuss these points and draw up mindmaps. Ask them to suggest endings for the example sentences in the *Useful language* box and clarify the grammar points as necessary.

5 Remind students that they looked at distinguishing fact from opinion in relation to reading in the previous unit, and that this is equally important in their own writing. For Exercise 5c, give them time to jot down supporting reasons before inviting a variety of statements.

6 Give students a few minutes to study the paragraph plan, and then check they know what should be included in the three sections. Ask for suggestions for completing the example sentences (e.g. *Nowadays, many families have more than one TV set, and it is common for children to have their own TV set in their bedroom*). Emphasise the academic nature of the task and the importance of register.

7 It would be useful to include the planning phase in class, if time permits, so that you can monitor weaker students' work.

KEY LANGUAGE
• **Cohesion: reference links** Exercise 10, page 193

Spot the error *(p.54)*

Remind students to note down the errors they've made in this task, and to make a point of studying the information in the *Error Hit List* very carefully. They should also be keeping a record of problem areas.

Unit 6 Key

Focus on vocabulary *(p.49)*
2 A Volleyball player **B** Chess player **C** Weight trainer **D** Guitarist **E** Kayaker

Focus on listening 1 *(p.50)*
1 Computer Studies **2** on campus **3** Film Society
4 (a) new gym **5** cooking **6** Jim Maybury
7 Athletics Club **8** a bit limited **9** (a) swimming pool **10** playing/plays the guitar

Focus on speaking *(p.50)*
1 three to four description points (the two *whats* can be combined) and one explanation point
2 (*Example answers*)
  1 Time **2** Benefits **3** Place **4** Equipment

Focus on listening 2 *(p.51)*
1 finishing time **2** lunch break **3** phone calls
4 wastepaper bin **5** (your/the) in-tray
6 outside work **7** listening to
8 watching television/TV **9** local community
10 musical instrument

Focus on writing *(p.52)*
3 (*Example answers*)
  1 lack of physical exercise, lack of social contact, lack of mental stimulation
  2 computer skills, learning through educational programmes, relaxation
  3 taking part in sporting activities (physical exercise), spending time with friends (socialisation), reading (reading skills and vocabulary building)
4 1 *because* is followed by a clause; *because of* is followed by a noun or pronoun
  2 *so* is followed by an adjective (without a noun) or by an adverb; *such* is followed by a noun (with or without an adjective)
5 a *arguably* (paragraph 1), *suggested* (paragraph 2)
  b (*Example answers*)
    The findings of a survey; the large number of workers who take time off for reasons of stress; the small percentage of junior managers who enjoyed their work.
  c (*Example answers*)
    • **One reason for this is** that they may spend the money unwisely. **Another (reason) is** that they won't develop a responsible attitude towards money.
    • **In the first place**, you can make and receive calls wherever you are. **In addition**, you don't need to have the right change to put in a call box.

Spot the error *(p.54)*
1 … on television … **2** … listen to the radio …
3 … watching television … **4** … playing the piano … **5** ✓ **6** … listen to the radio …
7 … concentrate on your driving … **8** ✓

7 ▶ The sound of music

TO SET THE BALL ROLLING ...

As a brief introduction, you could play a short piece of music (or draw a couple of musical notes on the board), and ask how important music is in students' lives. Find out what kind of memories/associations music evokes, e.g. music lessons as children, favourite singers, composers, films or TV programmes, even romance!

Use the Lead-in and Speaking sections to activate topic vocabulary, to practise social interchange and to tune students in to various aspects of the topic. The activities can easily take 30 minutes, so if time is limited, you will need to limit discussions and keep up a brisk pace.

Lead-in (p.56)

Check that students know the names of the instruments, and find out if anyone plays any of those shown. If necessary, remind them about the use of the definite article in *play the guitar* (*Error Hit List* Unit 6). Check understanding of *versatile* and elicit the noun *versatility* before they begin the discussion.

Afterwards, have a brief general discussion, ensuring that students justify their choices. It may also be worth introducing the names of the musicians (*drummer, guitarist,* etc.) since *flautist* occurs in the reading text.

Monitor pairwork as students discuss the remaining questions and invite brief feedback. You could also use one or more topics as the basis for an informal oral presentation to the class.

Focus on speaking 1 *Your tastes in music (p.56)*

Clarify any problems with terminology and give students a few moments to make their choices.

Focus attention on the *Useful language* box and, in particular, on the softeners (*So ..., I'm afraid ...,* etc.) and the adverbs. Practise as necessary, paying attention to appropriate stress and intonation, and then invite students to ask you a few questions about your tastes in music. It's worth pointing out that this language can be applied to a wide range of topics as well as music.

Arrange students in pairs or groups of three and monitor their conversations, noting any language which needs attention (e.g. you may have to point out that it's normal to speak about *jazz* rather than *jazz music*). To round off, ask a few students to report back on one of their partner's preferences.

NB When students check the results, you may want to explain that the survey, organised by the National Geographic Society in 2000, was the largest Internet-based survey ever undertaken at the time, with more than 80,000 participants from 178 countries.

Focus on reading *The sound of music (p.57)*

It's worth spending a little time on the issue of long texts and how to tackle them, since it is such a key exam skill. Ask students to suggest how long they think it takes to read a 900-word text, and if you feel the point needs emphasising, and you have time, get them to experiment with a text of roughly that length. The point is that detailed reading of three texts is simply not possible in the 60-minute time limit.

1 For this task, it's very important to set a time limit of just a few minutes. Hopefully, the right choice of answer will encourage students to trust the sampling approach. If students are in any doubt about the correct answer, encourage them to work towards it by eliminating the wrong answers. Emphasise the need to look at the text as a whole, and examine ways that wrong answers contain only partial truth.

2 Again, this should be done as quickly as possible.

3/4 Read through the introduction and make sure students are clear about the difference between False and Does Not Say answers. As a class, analyse the example given, and make sure students are quite clear about the reason for the Does Not Say answer. (Making the statement negative does not make it true. The text says that music is the most popular art form, but there is no mention of painting or any comparison between the two.) During the checking phase, make sure students justify their answers by reference to the text.

5/6 Check that students remember how to tackle this kind of task, and refer them back to the *Task approach* on page 29 if necessary. For each answer, tell them to jot down the paragraph number and underline the relevant parallel expression. (You may need to point less able students towards relevant paragraphs.) Reinforce this message during the checking phase, pointing out the importance of checking the text extremely carefully to be sure of the exact meaning. Clarify any points of usage as necessary, e.g. (F) *sensitive (to emotions)* applies to humans, not to music.

7 Talk through the introduction and *Task approach*, and stress the need to look for expressions which have the same meaning as phrases in the questions. When checking answers, ask students to identify the relevant paragraph and parallel expression, so as to eliminate any element of guesswork and underline the need for close, careful reading of the text.

Focus on vocabulary (p.61)

1/2/3 Talk through the introduction and discuss the meaning of *pivotal*. Then let students tackle Exercise 3, either in pairs or individually. If time is short or your students' vocabulary is relatively limited, stick to the general meanings listed in the Key. If you have time and your students are vocabulary-hungry, you could extend the discussion along the lines suggested in the Key.

4 Make sure students locate the expressions in the *Focus on reading* text and look carefully at the context when they do this task. The expressions which have obvious crossover relevance to the Writing paper are practised in a *Key language* exercise (see below).

5/6 The text contains some interesting compounds, and this provides an opportunity to focus on this aspect of word formation and, in particular, on a number of recent coinages like *know-how* and *downsize*. Exercise 6 is designed to show that it is usually relatively straightforward to guess the meanings of compound words.

KEY LANGUAGE

*   **Talking about research**
    Exercise 11, page 195

Focus on speaking 2 *Describing objects (p.63)*

1 Once the answers have been established, ask students to underline expressions used to describe size, shape and material, and focus on any other useful language, e.g. *They come in pairs.*

2 Point out that, when describing an object in the Speaking Test, it isn't necessary to use 'correct' technical vocabulary, as long as you can find a way of making it clear to the listener. Give students time to study the *Useful language* and point out that expressions like *roughly* and *sort of* and suffixes like *-ish* and *-y* can be particularly useful. With weaker students, you may want to elaborate further, e.g.

Colour: especially *light/dark* blue, *bright/dull* green, brow*nish*; *off-white*.

Material: especially *made of* versus *made from*, woo*den*, woo*llen*, leathe*ry*.

3 If you have time, you could usefully extend this activity to include objects in other categories, e.g. clothes, furniture, buildings.

4 Give students time to read the topic card, and remind them about the two key aspects: **describe** and **explain**. Make sure they all have notes to work from before beginning, and then monitor the pairwork. Give feedback to round off.

Unit 7 Key

Lead-in (p.56)

1 1 **A** drum kit   **B** saxophone   **C** violin
   D (grand) piano   **E** flute   **F** acoustic guitar
   G electric guitar   **H** trumpet

Focus on speaking 1 (p.56)

See Student's Book page 216.

Focus on reading (p.57)

1 B

3 1 F   The opposite is true; the text says *The existence of music mystifies scientists* (paragraph 1).

2 DNS We can't say for sure that the opposite is true. While the text doesn't say that Dr Atema played the instrument, it doesn't say he didn't either. It's therefore possible that he did (2).

3 DNS There is no mention of this.

4 F   The opposite is true: 'sad' music causes the temperature to <u>drop</u>. (3)

5 F   The opposite is true: male performers outnumbered female performers (by ten to one) (4).

6 DNS While Dr North says boys like rock and rap, he doesn't specifically say that girls don't (6).

7 DNS There is no mention of the book's success or otherwise (7).

8 F   The sacculus is not unique; it also exists in fish (9).

5 9 H   *... not a primary means of communication, unlike language* (paragraph 1)

10 A   *... human beings are the only species to make musical instruments* (1)

11 E   *... it had a range of less than one octave* (2)

12 G   *Psychologists are united in one belief – that music speaks to the heart.* (3)

13 B   *The peak age of the performers was 30* (4)

7 14 B   *musical talent ... can indicate many desirable qualities in a mate* (paragraph 5)

15 D   *music could vanish ... lifestyle would be virtually unchanged,* (7)

16/17   (in any order)
   A *Dr A's guess is that cavemen used the instrument to attract prospective mates* (2)
   B *GM ... thinks ... music ... was a factor in selecting a mate.* (4)

18 C   *While the girls listened to influence their mood ... boys used music ...* (6)

19 D   *... repetitive sounds appeal to the ear ...* (8)

Focus on vocabulary (p.61)

2 1 No   2 a wedding and a funeral   3 important

3 1 weak (NB also *a feeble joke, a feeble excuse*)

2 become slower or less active (other examples: *Our speed slackened as we approached the station; The demand for mobile phones has slackened in recent months.*)

3 avoids (usually through fear, dislike or lack of confidence)

4 agree with or support (particularly an opinion, belief or theory)

5 gives (a formal expression usually used in connection with honours, e.g. *An honorary degree was conferred on him.*)

6 (help to) explain

4 1 In fact,   2 After all   3 However   4 Yet
   5 What is more

5 1 (*Example*)   2 tone-deaf   3 birdsong
   4 signpost   5 know-how   6 lifestyle

6 1 idea or invention (especially a successful one)
   2 providing practical experience
   3 negative side
   4 favourable change
   5 reducing the number of staff

Focus on speaking 2 (p.63)

1 A eating (with); chopsticks
   B sewing/mending; a needle
   C calculating/adding up, etc.; a calculator

8 ▶ What's on

TO SET THE BALL ROLLING ...

Minimal introduction is needed, but you could ask when students last went to a cinema, theatre or concert, and briefly discuss cultural attractions in the town or city where you are.

Lead-in *(p.64)*

1 You may want to point out that there should be six words in each category. Ask students to compare their answers before checking and clarify meanings as necessary.

2 This is intended as a simple awareness-raising exercise, which can be built on as the course progresses. Being alert to word stress patterns is obviously relevant to speaking skills, but it is also an important listening skill.

   Most students will need a step-by-step introduction, beginning with practice in identifying the number of syllables. If so, begin with the one-syllable words from the list (eight including *on*), and then move on to two-syllable words (six) without differentiating between stress patterns in these. This will leave eight three-syllable words for students to work on. When you've checked the answers, practise these orally.

Focus on speaking 1 *Discussing cultural attractions (p.64)*

Focus first on the *Useful language*. Cleft sentences beginning *The thing ...* or *What ...* are common and useful structures, and most students would benefit from brief oral practice based on a different occasion (e.g. first day at work/school).

Divide students into pairs or groups. Monitor discussions and don't let them run on beyond their useful life. Afterwards, invite brief feedback.

Optional activities

1 (Pairs/groups) Ask students to explain which two cultural attractions they would recommend a visitor to their country to make a point of visiting, and why.

2 (Pairs) Give students the following list of museums and galleries (all in the London area). Ask them to work in pairs and each choose a museum they would like to visit. They should then explain to their partner the reasons for their choice and try to agree on an attraction to visit together.

pianos	postal history	Sigmund Freud
childhood	ethnology	contemporary art
taxicabs	butterflies	motor cars
astronomy	silk	maritime history

Focus on listening 1 *Music festival (p.65)*

Give students time to read through the *Task approach*, and to study the questions. It would be useful reinforcement to check the pronunciation of one or two items in the list (Question 1).

Focus on listening 2 *The Museum of Anthropology (p.66)*

Read through the *Exam briefing* together and check that students understand the terms *floor plan* and *cross-section*. Then ask them to study the diagram and check the word *ramp* (a slope connecting two levels). Point out that it doesn't necessarily matter if there are words on a diagram which they don't know. Thinking about them in advance will help them recognise these features when they hear them.

Give students time to study the other questions, making sure they are clear about the three other task types. Encourage them to think about the type of answer needed for each question in the first section, e.g. Question 1: a year; Question 2: a number; Question 3: *Yes* or *No*. When checking, read the section of the script containing the answers if necessary.

Focus on writing 1 *Describing tables (p.67)*

1/2 It's often useful to vary the way you describe statistics in tables and other diagrams, and this section practises a number of key expressions. Let students study the table and the example sentences before working through Exercises 1–2. You may want to point out that, despite the exercise rubric, there is only one possible match for item 6 in Exercise 2. NB There is a note on the expressions *one in ten* and *nine out of ten* in the *Error Hit List* for this unit.

3 Before students do Exercise 3, point out that qualifying expressions are equally useful in describing graphs and other diagrams where it's difficult to be precise about a figure.

4 Give students a few minutes to study the table, and then ask questions to check their reading of the table, e.g.:

- What does the table show? (attendance at cultural events in Great Britain)
- What is the timescale? (three specific years: 1987–88, 1991–92 and 1997–98)
- What do the figures in the table represent? (percentages)
- What was the most popular cultural attraction? (cinema)
- What were the least popular cultural attractions? (ballet, opera and contemporary dance)
- What has been the general trend over the period? (little change)
- Which cultural attraction is an exception to this trend? (cinema)
- In what way? (There's been a steady increase in cinema-going over the period.)

Give students time to complete the text and compare answers.

5 There are three practice tasks which can be tackled in class or set for homework as time allows (see below). One is a further gap-fill task of the kind above (*Writing practice*), another is an exercise focusing on cohesion (*Key language*) and the third is an exam-practice task with detailed *Task approach* (*Writing practice*).

WRITING PRACTICE

- **Describing information from a table (guided practice)**
  Exercise 2, page 208
- **Describing information from a table (exam task)**
  Exercise 3, page 209

Suggested approach for classwork
Whether done in class or set for homework, it's useful to read through the *Task approach* in class. To provide extra support, give students a few minutes to study the table, and then ask questions to check students' reading of the table, e.g.:
- What does the table show?
- What has been the overall trend in the number of visits to the UK? (a steady increase)
- How much has this increased over the period? (It's almost trebled.)
- Which is the most common reason for visiting the UK: business or leisure? (leisure)
- Where do most visitors to the UK come from: N. America or W. Europe? (W. Europe)
- How has the leisure sector changed over the period? (It's more than doubled.)
- How has the business sector changed over the period? (It's more than trebled.)
- Are both sectors still growing? (No, the leisure sector has decreased slightly.)

KEY LANGUAGE

- **Conditionals**
  Exercise 12, page 195

Focus on writing 2 *Presenting and justifying an opinion (p.68)*

1/2/3 It would be useful to give students practice with each set of expressions before they progress to Exercise 2. Make one or two more assertions to prompt each type of response, e.g. *Childhood is the happiest time of your life; Anyone who breaks the law deserves to go to prison.*

NB If you feel your students need practice in forming conditionals, ask them to do *Key language* Exercise 13 (see below) either before or after Exercise 3.

4 See if students can remember the basic approach to Task 2. If not, refer them back to the *Task approach* outlined on page 52. Ask students to read through the question and identify the key points. Discuss some possible reasons for disagreement, and some of the implications of the argument. It would be helpful to include the planning phase in class time if possible, so that students can exchange ideas and you can monitor their drafting of paragraph plans.

KEY LANGUAGE

- **Conditionals**
  Exercise 13, page 196

Focus on speaking 2 *Describing an event (p.70)*

1 See if students can identify the photos (fireworks over Sydney Harbour bridge and the Venice carnival) and use these as a springboard for this section. Monitor students' discussions, helping with vocabulary, as necessary, and have a brief round-up at the end.

2 Once students have read through the instructions, refresh their memories about the useful language (*The thing …, What ….* etc.) from *Focus on speaking 1*. The pairwork practice can be quite relaxed, and there's no need to set a time limit, but it's important to monitor students' performances and give feedback as necessary before they move on to Exercise 3.

3 Make sure everyone has decided on a topic and made some notes. You may want to set strict time limits, especially if the exam is looming, but if you can be more flexible, you may find that the discussion runs for quite a lot longer than the exam would allow. Afterwards, ask students to report briefly on what their partner described. Find out if there were any vocabulary 'gaps', and feed in any useful expressions that you've identified whilst monitoring.

Spot the error *(p.70)*

Remind students to note down the errors they've made in this correction task, and to make a point of studying the information in the *Error Hit List* very carefully. They should also be keeping a record of problem areas.

Unit 8 Key

Lead-in *(p.64)*

1 **Cinema:** subtitles, screen, stunt, on location, special effects, soundtrack.
   Theatre/Concert/Opera: stage, conductor, scenery, act, programme, dress rehearsal
   Museum/Gallery: sculpture, exhibit, collection, still life, landscape, catalogue
2 **A:** exhibit, collection, conductor, location, rehearsal
   B: cinema, opera, subtitle, scenery, catalogue

Focus on listening 1 *(p.65)*

1 C, E (in any order)   2 B   3 D   4 10.30 a.m.
5 £8   6 Africa Alive   7 lunch   8 £14.50
9 Bus Stop   10 (her) student card

Focus on listening 2 *(p.66)*

1 1949   2 one (1)   3 Yes   4 shop
5 information desk   6 (the) Great Hall
7 five (5) people   8 by bus / on a bus
9–10

	Mon	Tue	Wed	Thu	Fri	Sat	Sun
Winter	C	L					
Summer		L					

Focus on writing 1 *(p.67)*

1 1 a fifth / 20% were 'Very satisfied' and just over half / 50% were 'Satisfied'
   2 one per cent / one in 100
   3 five per cent / five in 100
2 1 a tenth / one in ten   2 a fifth / one in five
   3 a quarter / one in four   4 a third / one in three
   5 three quarters / three out of four
   6 nine out of ten (only possible answer)
3 1 just under half / 50%   2 one in three; (exactly) a third   3 just over half / 50%   4 approximately / about two thirds   5 less than ten per cent / fewer than one in ten   6 almost / approximately / about three quarters / 75%
4 (*Example answers*)
   1 6% / fewer than one in ten   2 just under a quarter / nearly one in four   3 not changed much
   4 about a third   5 more than half

Spot the error *(p.70)*

1 It is worth <u>pointing</u> out ...   2 There has been an increase <u>in</u> interest ...   3 ... is ~~a~~ good health ...
4 ✓   5 <u>At</u> the end of the period ...
6 It <u>may</u> be true ...   7 ✓   8 two and <u>a</u> quarter kilometres ...   9 ✓   10 ... <u>in</u> the end ...

9 ► Water, water everywhere

TO SET THE BALL ROLLING ...

Ask students to suggest a few of the world's valuable resources, e.g. gold, silver, oil and, hopefully, water. Then ask which is the most precious and why. Establish that life on Earth depends on water, and perhaps extend with a few trivia questions, e.g. *What percentage of water do our bodies contain?* (60–70%); *How long can human beings survive without water?* (no more than five to six days or two to three days in a hot climate).

Lead-in *(p.72)*

1 Use the first pair of activities as an example if necessary. You could also ask students to guess how many litres each activity uses. Then give them a couple of minutes to discuss the other pairs. As they check the answers, ask students to write the number of litres used next to each activity.

2 Read through the instructions and ask students to study the bar chart.

Ask a few questions to check that they can read it, e.g. *Which food is mentioned? How much water does it take to produce one serving of tomatoes? How many other foods are included in the chart?*

If necessary, help weaker students get started by directing them to the third or fourth sentences, which provide a comparison with tomatoes. After checking the answers, focus on key language. Ask students to underline the comparatives used in the four sentences, and then highlight these structures on the board, together with qualifiers. NB This language is also set out in *Key language* Exercise 7: *Numerical and other comparative expressions* on page 190.

nearly / (slightly) less than / (just) under (slightly) more than / (just) over / about / approximately

twice / three times <u>as much / many</u> ... <u>as</u>
50% <u>more</u> ... <u>than</u>
half / a quarter <u>of</u> / a third <u>of</u> ...

For further practice, you could ask students to compare: tomatoes/oranges; oranges/pasta; pasta/chicken.

3 There is plenty of scope for error with these comparatives, especially if students try to mix and match components (e.g. *a half more*). To avoid confusion and complicated explanations, encourage students to stick strictly to the three structures from the previous exercise.

Begin by eliciting endings for two example patterns, e.g.:
<u>Taking a shower uses</u> nearly twice as much water <u>as</u> <u>using a dishwasher</u>.
<u>It takes</u> over 50% more water to take a shower <u>than to</u> <u>use a dishwasher</u>.

Focus on the use of the verbs *take* and *use* (*It takes ... / X uses*), pointing out that they are not interchangeable, and also on the use of the *-ing* form and infinitive.

Add an additional example to remind students about the use of fractions, e.g.:
<u>Taking a shower</u> uses <u>three</u>-quarters of the water (which is) needed to take a bath.

Focus on speaking *Water issues (p.73)*

1 Depending on time, either answer these quickly as a class or in more depth as pairwork followed by class discussion.

2 NB You could usefully focus on **language of speculation** before students begin the quiz:
(I think) the answer could / might / may be ... because ...
For example ask: *Which country in the world has the highest ratio of cars to people?* (USA, with 570 cars to every 1,000 persons); *Where is the world's driest place?* (The Atacama Desert, Chile).

Tell students that even though they may not know the answers, they should discuss the options and choose the most likely answers.

Monitor students' conversations to make sure they are speculating and giving reasons. Afterwards, invite ideas on a few questions, without accepting or rejecting answers, since these can be found in the following text.

Focus on reading 1 *Water: Earth's most precious resource (p.74)*

NB Although a typical exam reading passage would not include information in tables in this way, the task is designed to practise skimming and scanning skills.

Read through the notes and then set students a time limit (say four to five minutes) to find the necessary information. When checking answers, ask students to identify the relevant section of text.

If time allows, you may want to exploit the figures for language practice and/or pick up on useful language, e.g. *to increase <u>sevenfold</u>, <u>by</u> 35 times, <u>by</u> more than half; <u>plentiful</u>; from a health <u>point of view</u>; <u>accounting for</u> as much as 80%.*

Focus on reading 2 *The Ecology of Hollywood (p.75)*

1/2 This is a long text so it's particularly important to reinforce the reading skills of skimming and scanning and to avoid lengthy intensive reading.

Remind students about the technique of sampling a text, which was introduced in Unit 7, and give them a few minutes to do so.

Let them read through the *Task approach* and study the table.

Give them time to scan the text and find and highlight the first topic (Los Angeles Aqueduct) before studying the information. You may need to help weaker students to locate the references to other aqueducts. As it's quite a challenging task, it's advisable to monitor students' work closely and give a helping hand, as necessary.

Let students compare answers before checking thoroughly, by reference to the text.

3 Read through the *Task approach* and let students study the question. Ask them to underline key words or phrases in each problem. Check vocabulary if necessary (e.g. *adverse, inadequate*).

They should have already highlighted the aqueducts, but will need to find and highlight the reference to *extraction* as well (paragraph 6).

Monitor students' work, helping as necessary, and ask them to underline the phrases in the text which match the problems.

Again, let them compare answers before checking thoroughly by reference to the text.

4 Sentence-completion tasks were introduced in Unit 3 (page 29). Read through the *Reminders*, and check that students follow the recommended procedure. Check answers thoroughly, by reference to the text.

Multiple-choice tasks were introduced in Unit 4 (page 45), and it's worth checking that students remember the *Task approach* before they begin. In particular, remind them of the three key questions: *Is it mentioned in the text? Is it true? Is it relevant?* You could help weaker students by telling them they need to focus on sections 8–10 of the text.

When checking answers, ask students to say why the wrong answers are wrong, i.e.

A Not true – waste <u>water</u> is being recycled. (para. 10)

D Not true – this was suggested (para. 8) but now the plan is to restore the river. (para. 9)

E Not true – the agencies already exist. (para. 9)

H Not mentioned in the text.

Focus on vocabulary *(p.79)*

NB The text contains a number of common expressions for introducing sentences such as *Surprisingly, Paradoxically* and *Inevitably*. These and other expressions are practised in 16 *Key language* Exercise 16 (see below).

1 The aim is to encourage students to make intelligent guesses about the meaning of difficult or unusual words and expressions. Make sure students do look for the expressions in the text and study the context, rather than simply guess. When checking, clarify meaning and use with extra examples, as necessary.

2 In some cases, it's easy to say which noun or verb the adjective is derived from (e.g. *ecology/ecological*), but in others, the derivation is less transparent. This exercise is best done in class, since students can then be encouraged to add to the list and/or suggest other topic areas, particularly from their own specialisation. NB There is also *Key language* practice in this area of language (see below).

KEY LANGUAGE

- **Derived adjectives and nouns**
  Exercises 14 and 15, page 197
- **Introducing sentences**
  Exercise 16, page 197

Unit 9 Key

Lead-in (p.72)

1 See Student's Book page 217.

2 The missing foods, from left to right: oranges, pasta, milk, chicken.

3 (*Example answers*)

1 Taking a bath uses more than 30% more water than taking a shower.
2 It takes seven times more water to use a dishwasher than to wash dishes by hand.
3 We use ten times as much water for cooking each day as for drinking.
4 It takes over three times as much water to water the garden as to wash the car. / Washing the car uses less than a third of the water needed to water the garden.

Focus on speaking (p.73)

2 1 b) (Figure 2)
2 80 (Text after Figure 3)
3 USA, Japan (highest); India (lowest) (Figure 3)
4 70% (Text after Figure 1)
5 e.g. glaciers, aquifers, lakes, rivers, atmosphere, biosphere. (Figure 1)
   NB It's worth introducing the term *aquifer*, since it occurs again in the main text: an *aquifer* is any rock formation containing water that can be used to supply wells.
6 a) (Text after Figure 1)
7 c) (Text after Figure 4)
8 a) (most); b) (least) (Figure 4)

Focus on reading 2 (p.75)

2 1 1941 (para. 5)   2 350km (4)   3 *not given*
4 Mono Lake (5)

3 5 C *Within ten years, the city needed more.* (para. 5)
6 E *LA was ordered to reduce its water intake …* (5)
7 A *with the water level in Mono Lake falling to dangerously low levels* (5)
8 E *LA's entitlement was reduced by about 50%* (5)
9 B *with inevitably harmful consequences for fish and wildlife* (5)
10 D *40 per cent of wells … contaminated above federal limits* (6)

4 11 H (para. 1)
12 J *respiratory problems due to vehicle emissions* (2)
13 A *No metropolis on the planet has looked further afield for its supply* (4)
14 I (5)
15 G *the considerable winter rainfall … is swallowed by concrete drainage systems …* (6)
16 B *a threat to economic expansion* (7)
17–20 (in any order)
B *nature walks … equestrian trails* (9)
C *to collect run-off rainwater from buildings and redirect it …* (10)
F *to restore the river* (9)
G *recreate wetland areas to attract birds* (9)

Focus on vocabulary (p.79)

1 1 d 2 e 3 a 4 c 5 b
2 1 F 2 H 3 G 4 A 5 C 6 D 7 E 8 B

10 ▶ Hazard warning

TO SET THE BALL ROLLING ...

It's useful to begin by clarifying terms (with books closed). Ask students to give an example of a natural hazard (e.g. earthquake) and establish that it is an extreme natural event, which is likely to cause serious loss of life and destruction of property when it occurs in a populated area. Ask students to think of more examples and to suggest two or three main categories, according to cause (climatic, geological, land instability). Point out that the topic, which crosses several disciplines, including geography and geology, is an increasingly popular field of study.

NB It has been estimated that natural hazards are responsible for 250,000 deaths and US$40 billion of damage each year.

Lead-in *(p.80)*

1 a Clarify any vocabulary students are unsure about. For *tsunami*, see the cartoon. Should students ask, *tropical cyclones* are the same as *hurricanes* and *typhoons* (violent revolving storms with high winds, usually occurring in the tropics). *Tornados* are swirling columns of wind, common in the central USA. Allow a few minutes for the discussion, and then invite brief feedback.

b Use the checking phase to clarify vocabulary and/or elaborate further, as necessary.

2 NB It may be helpful for students to practise expressions of cause and result before beginning this task (see *Key language*, Exercise 17).

Make sure students understand the concept of grading natural hazards in terms of the severity of their impact, and discuss each of the factors briefly beforehand. Invite feedback after the pairwork, and develop the discussion to include relevant issues and vocabulary, such as warning time, population density (*densely/ sparsely populated*), and effects on infrastructure (*communication failures; closure of schools and airports,* etc.). Finally reveal (or let students refer to) the official ranking on page 217. If you have time, you could use the table for practice in interpreting statistical information, e.g.: *Which events – cause the greatest loss of life? – affect the largest area? – have the greatest social effect?*

KEY LANGUAGE

- **Expressing cause and result:** *cause, result in, lead to; result from, as a result of*
  Exercise 17, page 198
This exercise practises a number of expressions which are useful in talking and writing about this topic. Given the possible pitfalls where grammar is concerned, the exercise is probably best done in class, except with very able students.

Focus on listening 1 *Predicting a volcanic eruption (p.81)*

Before playing the recording, allow time for studying and/or discussing the drawing, either in pairs or as a class, and invite a few guesses as to possible answers.

If you have time when checking answers, you could focus on a few interesting expressions, e.g. *I'll have to take your word for it; if I remember rightly.*

NB The recording script provides an opportunity to focus on *the … the …* comparatives (*The bigger it is, the more likelihood there is of an eruption*), which are practised in *Key language* Exercise 20, page 201. However, this language point is referenced in Unit 12, and you may prefer to wait until then.

Focus on listening 2 *Tsunami (p.82)*

Remind students about the importance of scanning instructions and questions in advance when there are several task-types like these, and you need to adapt quickly.

Give students time to study the diagram and list. Check they can remember the key points of advice for labelling a diagram (if not, ask them to refer to the *Exam briefing* on page 66) and that they recognise the main features: sea level, sea floor and the (schematic) waves. Make sure they notice how the numbers run (clockwise).

Check pronunciation of the words in the list A–F, and remind students of the advice from Unit 8: to say words silently in advance so they are easier to recognise on the recording.

If you have time when checking answers, you could focus on one or two useful expressions, e.g. *mean* (= average), *one-storey* (+ *single-storey, two-storey, multi-storey*).

Focus on writing *Describing a process (p.83)*

1 Give students time to read through the *Exam briefing* and *Task approach*, and then test their recall (e.g. *How many task-types are possible for Task 1 of the Writing module? When do you need to divide a description into paragraphs?*)

2 After establishing the correct answer, ask students to study the diagram again and suggest a suitable starting point for the description (there's no particular need for consensus on this), and then to attempt to describe it simply in their own words. Clarify vocabulary and revise the use and formation of the passive, if necessary (*Key language* Exercise 5, page 188).

3/4 With weaker students it may help to go through the first two questions as a class to illustrate the kind of choices of verb form they need to make, i.e. singular/plural? active/passive?

5/6 The aim is to raise student awareness of, and encourage appropriate use of, a good range of sequence markers. These should be given a high profile throughout the rest of the unit, both in writing and speaking sections. NB *At first/first, at last/lastly* and *after/afterwards* feature in the *Error Hit List* in this unit.

7 Allow time for students to study the diagram and ask any questions. Remind them to try and put the notes on the diagram into their own words where possible. They should write their answer as a single paragraph of about 80–100 words, linking sentences appropriately (as practised in Unit 2) and marking stages with suitable sequence expressions. With weaker students, it may be helpful to run through the description orally first.

NB There is a further gapped model description in the *Writing practice* (Exercise 4), which you may want to use for extra practice before students progress to the exam task. Alternatively, this could be reserved for revision at a later stage.

8 Although the diagram may look a bit complicated, the process should be fairly easy to follow and the necessary topic vocabulary is supplied. It would help to talk through the sequence beforehand, making sure students are aware that there are two separate processes (making the pencil leads and making the pencil cases). These come together at the point where the leads are inserted into the wooden slats.

Discuss whether there needs to be more than one paragraph (one is acceptable, but two may be clearer), and remind them of the importance of good linking with appropriate sequence expressions.

With weaker students, you may need to practise describing the process orally first. If students still need help, use the example answer in the Key to give prompts or to prepare a gapped model.

WRITING PRACTICE

- **Describing a process**
  Exercise 4, page 210

Focus on speaking *Sequencing (p.86)*

1 These topics provide an opportunity to use sequence expressions in speaking. You could remind students of the list on page 84, but point out that the following are quite formal and therefore normally restricted to written English: *subsequently, at this stage* and *during this process*. It's a good idea to give an example of what is required first, taking a different topic, e.g. 'How I became an English language teacher'.

2 This activity usually generates a lot of discussion and some surprising results!

Make sure students understand the instructions and task before they begin. If you have access to an OHP and can prepare a transparency of the official table on page 217, the answers can be revealed bit by bit, for dramatic effect. Afterwards discuss people's tendency to underestimate voluntary everyday risks, and overestimate more dramatic involuntary risks like floods. What reasons could there be for this?

NB This topic can also be exploited for writing (see *Writing practice* below).

WRITING PRACTICE

- **Presenting and justifying an opinion (exam task)**
  Exercise 5, page 211

Spot the error *(p.86)*

Remind students to note down the errors they've made in correction, and to make a point of studying the information in the *Error Hit List* very carefully. They should also be keeping a record of problem areas so that these can be revised regularly and, hopefully, eliminated! This task will check students' revision as it recycles some errors from earlier Hit Lists.

Unit 10 Key

Lead-in (p.80)

1 b Volcano: active, erupt, crater, extinct, dormant
Earthquake: tremor, aftershock, seismic, fault line, epicentre

2 See Student's Book page 217.

Focus on listening 1 (p.81)

1 height (of cloud)
2 volume (of cloud)
3 drying vegetation
4 landslide
5 mudflow
6 earthquake
7 wells drying (up)
8 abnormal animal behaviour
9 rumbling (sound)
10 sulphur smell

Focus on listening 2 (p.82)

1 C
2 E
3 D
4 earthquake(s)
5 80–90%
6 half a / 0.5 metre
7 Russia
8 480km
9 700
10 B

Focus on writing (p.83)

2 B

3 1 causes (the) 2 is released 3 rises 4 are blown
5 reach 6 fall 7 is absorbed 8 runs

4 Present simple and present perfect simple tenses; because we are referring to events which happen repeatedly, all the time.

5 As, then, until, At this stage, After, eventually

6 1 Meanwhile, During this process, At this stage
2 Eventually
3 *First, Finally*: because they indicate the beginning and end of a process, which is inappropriate for a cycle, as it is continuous.

7 (*Example answer*)
Carbon is used repeatedly in a process called the carbon cycle. Plants take in carbon dioxide from the air through their leaves. Animals **then** feed on plants, absorbing carbon dioxide, which they **later** release into the atmosphere by breathing. When plants and animals die, they decompose and their remains are **subsequently** absorbed into the ground. Over millions of years, fossil fuels such as coal, oil or natural gas are formed. **Eventually**, these fossil fuels are burnt as a source of energy and, **during this process**, carbon dioxide is given off.

8 (*Example answer*)
Pencils are made from graphite and wood. During the manufacturing process, ground graphite is **first** mixed with clay and water to make a dough. **Once** the dough has reached the required consistency, it is passed through a forming press and emerges as a long, thin rod. This rod is **then** cut into pencil-length pieces called leads, and these are allowed to dry. **After** drying, the leads are placed in an oven and heated to 800 degrees Celcius.
Meanwhile, the pencil case is prepared. Wood is sawn into wide slats, and a number of grooves are cut lengthwise into each one. **Next**, a layer of glue is applied, and a pencil lead is placed in each groove. Another slat is **then** placed on top, making a sandwich. **Finally**, the slats are separated into individual pencils, and these are sent through a shaping machine to create a smooth finish. The pencils are then ready for use. (154 words)

Spot the error (p.86)

1 ✓
2 Firstly/First/First of all …
3 … economical …
4 … later/afterwards …
5 ✓
6 At first …
7 … an increase in …
8 a large/considerable/substantial amount …
9 … on the television …
10 ✓

11 ▶ Use it or lose it

TO SET THE BALL ROLLING ...

Ask students to think of something they have to remember that day (e.g. a phone call to make, a bill to pay, where they parked the car!). Elicit a few examples and briefly discuss strategies for remembering these things. You could also elicit some topic vocabulary, e.g. *be forgetful/absent-minded, have a memory/mind like a sieve; learn by heart, have a photographic memory, jog someone's memory.*

NB This teaching unit (whether covered in one session or more) works particularly well if it is framed by the two parts of the Memory Test. Leaving the last five to ten minutes for Part 2 requires careful timing, but is worthwhile.

Lead-in *(p.88)*

1/2 Start with books closed. Explain how the Memory Test will work, and check that everyone is clear about what they have to do. Tell them they can write words down on a piece of paper if they think this will help. For fairness, ensure that students start and stop studying the words simultaneously. Time the two minutes as exactly as possible.

It may be worth checking students' lists quickly afterwards to make sure there are no wrong words or wildly wrong spellings. Ask them to make a note of their score for future reference before talking through the discussion points as a class.

3 Encourage students to think of other methods apart from making a written note. Invite feedback after pairwork, and perhaps list a range of strategies on the board. It's worth spending a bit of time on the last item as a way of highlighting effective strategies for remembering new vocabulary (e.g. recording expressions in a context, a phrase or sentence, rather than in isolation; making a point of revising and using new expressions; grouping words in word families).

If time allows, you could extend the discussion of some of the points and introduce extra vocabulary, e.g. *impulse buying.*

Focus on reading 1 *Sleep (p.89)*

1 It may be easiest to discuss the headline if it's written on the board. Otherwise, ask students to cover the article. Check *eve* and *sleep* (noun or verb?) and invite speculation about the general meaning. Afterwards, explain the phrase *to burn the midnight oil*, i.e. to work or study until late at night.

2 Set a time limit for reading of about a minute, to discourage detailed reading.

3 Set a time limit of about two minutes to reinforce the key element of scanning.

4 You may need to do the first question together, so as to underline the need for an exact match of cause and effect, and also for consistency of tenses. When checking, ask students to justify answers by reference to the text. Question 3 in particular will repay analysis, since it relies on understanding several reference links (see the Key).

NB If you have time, you could also look at some vocabulary use in the text, e.g.:

* **metaphorical expressions**, e.g. *to **cram** for an exam* = study hard and quickly (compare *to cram things into a suitcase*); ***crippling** effects* = damaging or weakening (compare *a cripple/to cripple*); *to **nail** something **down*** = fix it permanently

* **dependent prepositions**, e.g. *to deprive people of sleep, to substitute study for sleep*

Focus on reading 2 *Use it or lose it (p.90)*

1 You may want students to work through all the questions without interruption, especially if the exam is close. If you feel the class needs more support, however, follow the suggested approach on the next page.

2 Let students read through the *Exam briefing*, and then give them a limited time (four minutes, say) to answer the questions. Ask them to compare answers before checking.

Optional activity: To allow students to explore the topic further before continuing with the exam questions, write the three categories *Mental Speed, Learning Capacity* and *Working Memory* on the board. Let students find and study the information about these in the text, and then ask them to discuss which would be involved in the following:

1 using a sophisticated new camera;
2 doing the shopping in a big supermarket;
3 deciding what to do when a frying pan catches fire;
4 finding out how to use the Internet;
5 playing a doubles game at tennis;
6 making arrangements for a children's party.

3 Check that students remember how to tackle this task. (If not, refer them to the *Task approach* on page 29.) Make sure they underline key words or phrases as they look through the questions (check these if necessary), and ask them to note down the number of the relevant paragraph next to their chosen answer. Check answers together with paragraph references.

4 Let students read through the *Reminders* and highlight the people A–C in the text. Don't point out that A appears twice – deal with this at the checking stage if necessary. Remind students that Statements 7–11 are likely to paraphrase information from the text. When checking, ask students to quote relevant paragraph numbers.

For the True/False/Does Not Say section, remind students, if necessary, that questions are in the same order as the information in the text. When checking, make sure students can justify their answers by reference to the text.

Focus on vocabulary *Word families (p.93)*

This task is suitable for homework. Remind students of the value of learning vocabulary in sets.

NB The text also provides an opportunity to focus on semi-fixed phrases (i.e. phrases where it's possible to make small variations by adding adjectives and adverbs), and if you have time, you could also look at some of these, e.g.:

> *(partly)* **explains why/how** … (paragraph 2)
> **provides** *(even stronger)* **evidence of** … (8)
> **lead to / point to the** *(interesting/intriguing/worrying)* **possibility of/that** … (10)
> **has** *(clearly)* **shown** *that* … (10)

Focus on speaking *Memories (p.94)*

1 Give students the necessary time checks and monitor their work. Perhaps pick out one or two to present their topic to the class afterwards.

2 You may want to revise relevant language before (or after) the task, e.g. *When I was a child / X years ago,* + past tense; *Since then / Over the last few years* + present perfect. Again, time checks are required.

3 As with Part 1 of the Memory Test, it's best to run through the instructions with books closed. You can then ensure that everyone has exactly two minutes to study the diagrams. Ask students to total their scores for the two parts and see if anyone had significantly better results in one or other part. If time allows, you could check some related language, e.g. *shaped like a rectangle, roughly rectangular in shape.*

4 Monitor pairwork and have a general round-up discussion, touching on topics like verbal versus visual awareness (Question 1), and effective exam preparation (Questions 2 and 3).

KEY LANGUAGE

- **Articles**
  Exercise 18, page 199

Unit 11 Key

Focus on reading 1 *(p.89)*

3 1 the link between sleep and memory

2 Harvard Medical School
3 in *Nature Neuroscience* (a scientific journal)
4 24
5 a visual discrimination task (involving diagonal lines on a computer screen)

4 1 E (first and second paragraphs)
2 F (whole article)
3 D *Those* (volunteers) who *had not* (slept normally), showed *none* (no improvement)
4 B To eliminate the effects of fatigue … then slept normally …
5 A Among the group who had slept normally, … a marked improvement.
6 C (last paragraph)

Focus on reading 2 *(p.90)*

2 1 B, C, E (in any order)
3 2 C (para. 2) **3** F (3) **4** A (5) **5** H (5)
  6 D (8)
4 7 A (7) **8** C (10) **9** A (2) **10** B (8)
11 C (10)
12 TRUE (4/5) Absentmindedness occurs at all ages; Stress … can also cause such absentmindedness
13 TRUE (8)
14 FALSE (10) mental not physical training
15 DNS
16 FALSE (11) Why this should be true for memory … is not yet clear

Focus on vocabulary *(p.93)*

1 suspicion **2** suspicious **3** decision **4** decisive
5 comparison **6** comparative/comparable
7 lengthen **8** length **9** benefit **10** beneficial
11 age **12** ageing/aged **13** memorise (-ize US)
14 memorable **15** variety/variation
16 various/variable

12 ▶ You live and learn

TO SET THE BALL ROLLING ...

You could discuss one or more of the following quotations:

- *... it is well to remember from time to time that nothing that is worth knowing can be taught.* (Oscar Wilde, Irish playwright and poet)

- *Education is what most people receive, many pass on and few have.* (Karl Kraus, Austrian critic)

- *Education is what survives when what has been learnt has been forgotten.* (B.F. Skinner, American psychologist)

Lead-in *(p.95)*

Education is one of the most predictable topics in the Speaking Test, so it's important that students are clear about relevant vocabulary, particularly expressions relating to their own studies, whether in the past or planned for the future. Be prepared to add vocabulary that is specific to your students' needs.

1/2 Let students discuss these two tasks and clarify any meanings, as necessary.

- *Fresher* = a student in their first year of study (British English). The US equivalent is *freshman*.

- *Thesis* = a long piece of writing, based on original work, usually prepared for a university postgraduate degree. NB This word occurs in *Focus on writing* 2 with a second and less common meaning: an opinion supported by a reasoned argument.

3 Word stress was introduced in Unit 8. If students still need practice in identifying syllables, use the examples as a starting point. Then, from the list in Exercise 1, ask them to identify two one-syllable words and a few two- and three-syllable words. Once they're reasonably confident, move on to stress, going back to the examples for practice. When you've checked the answers, practise these orally as well.

It's worth reading through the *Language fact* box in class to make sure the pattern is clear. You could also give oral practice using the following words:

- *technology sociology meteorology criminology*
- *variety complexity electricity probability*
- *geography demography radiography oceanography philosophy*
- *librarian humanitarian parliamentarian*
- *geometry symmetry*
- *educate calculate exaggerate discriminate*
- *astronomy economy agronomy*

Focus on speaking 1 *Schooldays (p.96)*

1 Point out the difference between giving answers which are <u>adequate</u> in Part 1 of the test and answers which are <u>excellent</u>. Emphasise the importance of really listening to the question (not giving a prepared answer to a similar question), and using the opportunity to demonstrate a good range of structures and vocabulary.

2 Practise forming questions from the prompts beforehand if necessary. You could also ask one or two preliminary questions to practise the *Useful language*, e.g. *Which was your least favourite subject at school? Why?* or *Who was your best friend at school? What was special about them?*

3 Give students time to study the topics and make notes. Remind them, if necessary, to use key words or phrases (possibly set out in a mindmap) rather than sentences. Monitor, making sure monologues don't slip into dialogues. Afterwards ask a few students to explain briefly what their partners said, and give any relevant language feedback.

Focus on listening 1 *The golden rules of listening (p.97)*

1 Use the questionnaire as a springboard for a brief discussion about listening skills: what helps, what hinders, how to improve, etc. Then let students look through the tasks, and perhaps discuss a few possible answers as a way of encouraging prediction as a routine strategy.

Note on the cartoon: Diogenes was a Greek philosopher who became legendary for his rejection of life's comforts – he was reputed to have lived for a time in a barrel.

2 The recording script contains a number of common collocations, including simple verbs such as *pay attention* and *make a good impression*. If you have time, you could include *Key language* Exercise 19, which practises similar collocations. Encourage students to keep a careful record of those they slip up on.

KEY LANGUAGE
• **Vocabulary: collocations** Exercise 19, page 201

Focus on listening 2 *Making the most of your memory (p.98)*

1/2 Take time to discuss pre-listening Questions 1–5 as a class (without providing definitive answers) and point out how important it is to be alert for clues like these.

3 These questions encourage students to reflect on the task and on strategies they used. You could also ask if there was any information in the lecture which they feel they could make use of in their own learning.

NB The recording script contains an example of a *the … the* comparative. There is optional practice in this area of language in *Key language* Exercise 20.

KEY LANGUAGE
• *The … the* (comparatives) Exercise 20, page 201

Focus on speaking 2 *Teachers and children (p.99)*

You may want to revise relevant language before students discuss these mini topics, e.g. *In my opinion, As I see it, On the one hand … on the other*. Alternatively, you could adopt a Test, Teach, Test approach, where you revise language as necessary on the basis of students' performance. You could also develop one or two topics into a class discussion, if time allows.

Focus on writing 1 *Presenting an opinion (p.99)*

1 This task introduces the *thesis-led* approach as an alternative to the *argument-led* approach which was discussed in Unit 6. It also looks at linking ideas using expressions of concession or contrast.

2 Briefly discuss students' initial reactions to the exam topic. Give them time to highlight key words or phrases in the question and make notes. If more help is needed, you could talk through some of the issues as a class first, e.g. *What is the purpose of testing (for students and teachers)? What kind of things could teachers do instead if they didn't have to concentrate on exam preparation?*

3/4/5 Begin by revising the basic structure of an *argument-led* approach. It may be helpful to clarify the meaning of *thesis* here (i.e. an opinion put forward and supported by a reasoned argument), as distinct from its more common meaning discussed earlier in the *Lead-in*. Make sure students are clear about how the two approaches differ, and which situations they are best suited to. Monitor the paragraph planning and let students compare results afterwards.

6/7/8/9 Read through the examples and discuss the questions as a class. For Exercise 7, point out that sentences can be combined or not, depending on which linking expression is chosen. It may be helpful to do the first together to illustrate the various possible answers. Ask students to re-read the *Reminders* on page 99 before they begin the exam-practice task.

Focus on writing 2 *Diagrams and tables (p.101)*

This task focuses on the importance of selecting key information from a detailed diagram. It also looks at the need to vary the expressions used in a description to avoid too much repetition.

1/2 Ask students to read through the *Reminders* and then study the exam task and diagram on page 102.

Establish that it would be neither appropriate nor possible in 150 words to describe all the information in the diagram. Ask what the main points of interest are, i.e. pupils' general strengths and weaknesses across subjects, and also any significant differences of performance by boys and girls in individual subjects.

Let students do Exercises 1 and 2. Before they tackle the exam task, you may want to revise ways of reporting statistics and rounding up to the nearest figure (page 67) and possibly some of the *numerical and other comparative expressions* from *Key language* Exercise 7, page 190.

For Questions 5 and 6 in Exercise 2, make sure they understand that they should first identify the two subjects in which girls/boys did significantly better, then use the subject in which the *difference* between the sexes was greatest to draw comparisons.

NB There is a gapped model answer for this task (see below).

WRITING PRACTICE
• **Interpreting statistics (guided practice)** Exercise 6, page 211

Unit 12 Key

Lead-in (p.95)

1 School (S): headmaster, class, pupil, detention, form, lesson, homework, secondary, teacher
College/University (U): professor, degree, lecturer, undergraduate, tutorial, seminar, fresher, thesis, campus

2 1 a) one of (usually) three periods into which the school or university year is divided, especially in Britain
   b) one of (usually) two periods into which the university year is divided, especially in the US and Australia
2 a) a section of a university or other large organisation, dealing with a particular subject or subjects, e.g. Department of Maths and Science
   b) a group of related departments in a college or university, e.g. Faculty of Arts
   Also all the lecturers in a particular faculty.
3 a) all the courses of study offered in a school, college or university
   b) an arrangement of subjects for a particular course of study

3 A *pupil, lesson, teacher, homework, fresher, thesis, campus* (<u>not</u> *degree* o O)
B *headmaster, professor, detention, semester department*
C *seminar, secondary, lecturer, faculty, syllabus*

Focus on listening 1 (p.97)

1 See Student's Book page 217.
2 1, 2 B, E (in any order)
   3 familiar
   4 tense and/or anxious / feeling / tense/anxious
   5 full attention
   6 to make notes
   7 your judgement
   8 feeling
   9 win (an) argument
   10 is not saying / does not say

Focus on listening 2 (p.98)

1 Storage
2 Verbal
3 Preview
4 State
5 through it quickly
6 review the contents
7 paying attention
8 make (any) mistakes
9 know well
10 A

Focus on writing 1 (p.99)

4 1 In an *argument-led* approach, you only state your overall conclusion at the end, after evaluating all the evidence. In a *thesis-led* approach, you begin by stating your point of view and then set out reasons to justify this.
   2 a *thesis-led* approach
   3 an *argument-led* approach

6 1 *despite / in spite of* are followed by a noun group; *although* is followed by a subordinate clause.
   2 *however, nevertheless, on the other hand*
   3 *on the other hand*

7 (*Example answers*)
   1 **Despite the fact that** football hooligans receive a lot of publicity, there are millions of spectators who cause no trouble at all.
   2 **While** many people feel that censorship is unacceptable in a free society, it's undeniable that children need some form of protection from *unsuitable subject matter*.
   3 **Although** medical advances are extending the human lifespan, not everyone wants *to live to be 100*.
   4 Smoking is known to cause *lung cancer and other serious diseases*. **Nevertheless**, people have the right to *make their own health decisions*.
   5 City life undoubtedly has many advantages such as *convenient shopping and leisure facilities*. **On the other hand**, city dwellers face many problems, including *crime and pollution*.

8 (*Example answers*)
   1 <u>While</u> the economic situation …
   2 Despite <u>the fact that</u> / <u>Even though</u> I agree …
   3 … in spite <u>of</u> the fact …
   4 Although modern vaccines … ~~but~~ …

Focus on writing 2 (p.101)

2 1 English and Mathematics
   2 Biology, Chemistry and Physics
   3 Mathematics, Biology
   4 English (61.5%, well over half)
   5 English and French (The girls' pass rate in French was over / more than 50% higher than the boys'.)
   6 Craft, Design and Technology and Physics (The boys' pass rate in Physics was almost double / twice that of the girls.)

3 1 get poor results   **2** almost double   **3** do well
   4 percentage of successful candidates   **5** figure
   6 much   **7** equal   **8** roughly

13 ▶ Bones to phones

TO SET THE BALL ROLLING ...

As a brief introduction, sketch a letter, telephone and computer on the board and ask which is most useful for communication. Alternatively, ask students to jot down all the ways they have communicated, apart from speaking, in the last 24 hours, nudging them if necessary into extending the basic list of notes, e-mail, etc. to include facial expression, gesture and even sounds (sighs, groans, laughs, etc.). Point out that the singular of *media* (of communication) is *medium*.

Lead-in *(p.104)*

1 This task encourages students to consider communications in broad terms and to think about some basic distinctions between various (mainly visual) systems. For interest, approximate dates of invention are included in the Key.

The task can be done fairly quickly, but if students are interested and time allows, you could usefully develop the topic discussion to include some of the points below. This works well if you have an OHP and can make a transparency of items A–H.

NB There are two basic types of writing system: *phonological* (representing sounds) – the majority of those used today – and *non-phonological* – as used in the earliest writing systems. Non-phonological symbols range from recognisable representations of objects *(pictograms)* as in C, to more abstract symbols standing for words, as in G. You could mention that the Chinese character for 'man' written three times stands for group, while 'woman' written twice stands for 'quarrel'!

2 To give the discussion more focus, ask students to try and agree on their answers. Make sure they justify their answers to b.

Focus on reading 1
Communication devices *(p.105)*

1 Give students time to read the texts and discuss ideas together. If need be, point out a few clues, e.g. **A** *digital networks, fashion accessory;* **B** *began to be worn, Switzerland;* **D** *send and receive pictures, office use*. When checking, ask students to say which information helped them. You could also ask students to imagine they could only have one of the five inventions, and say which they would choose, and why.

2 For greater clarity, introduce each type of participle clause and its meaning on the board (or OHP) first. It may be helpful to point out that the term *-ed* in *-ed* clauses refers to all past participles, whether they end in *-ed* or not. Perfect participles e.g. *Having remained*, may need special attention – make sure students realise they are *-ing* (rather than *-ed*) forms.

3/4 This is an important language area, which should be reinforced regularly by asking students to identify participle clauses in reading texts.
NB For practice in using the most common verbs in participle clauses, see below.

KEY LANGUAGE

- **Common verbs in *-ed* and *-ing* clauses**
  Exercise 21, page 202

Focus on reading 2 *Bones to phones (p.106)*

1 Before they begin, ask students to read the heading and introduction to the reading text (*Radio survived …*) and briefly speculate about the content of the article.

2 Remind students about the two kinds of heading task (see Student's Book page 42). Then, following the *Task approach*, focus on the example. Ask students to cover Questions 1–8, then read paragraph C and choose the best answer (xii). When checking answers, make sure students can justify their answers by reference to the text.

3 Ask students to underline or highlight in the text the ten media listed in the box. Again, use the example as a way of reviewing this task-type. Ask students to read the information about missile mail (paragraph E in the text) and pinpoint the information which **matches the note** (*Before man reaches the Moon, … guided missile*).

4 Elicit the three key questions from the *Task approach* on page 45. (Is it mentioned in the article? Is it true? is it relevant?) When checking, make sure students can justify their answers by reference to the text where possible.

Focus on vocabulary *Introducing examples (p.110)*

The expressions are not interchangeable, so check that students are clear about when to use each one, and draw their attention to relevant punctuation features. If you have time, you may want to explore this language area in more depth, by looking at common collocations, e.g. *a good/typical/striking/glaring example*, or by adding extra expressions, e.g. *... a (good) case in point.*

NB If you have time for more vocabulary study, you could also focus on the use of the word *doubt*, which occurs in the text, and set the *Key language* exercise below for class or homework.

KEY LANGUAGE
• **Doubt**   Exercise 22, page 202

Focus on speaking *Comparing and contrasting (p.110)*

1 Treat the first question as a general discussion, using the students' own experience of these media as far as possible. To provide greater focus, ask them which they would use for specific purposes, such as breaking up with a boy/girlfriend, applying for a job, arranging a party at short notice, closing a bank account, keeping in touch with friends abroad.

2 To set the ball rolling, discuss one or two more notes which could be added under *letter* (e.g. delayed feedback, pictures/documents can be enclosed). Then let students complete the mindmap, before inviting brief feedback.

3 Before the pairwork, it may be helpful to practise the *Useful language* orally, using the mindmap notes, and/or ways of expressing personal preferences (e.g. *I much prefer using the telephone to writing a letter*). Provide time checks for the long turns.

Unit 13 Key

Lead-in *(p.104)*

1 A Sign language (1775, France) – hand movements representing letters or words

B Morse code (1837, USA) – groups of long or short sounds representing a letter

C Egyptian hieroglyphics (c. 3000 BC) – picture signs indicating words

D symbols indicating washing instructions (modern)

E Shorthand (Pitmanscript, 1837) – a system of speedwriting

F Hindi script – each letter representing a sound, as in English

G Chinese characters (c. 1700 BC) – abstract symbols representing words

H mathematical symbols

1 Morse code (not a written medium). Other answers are possible.

2 They both represent recognisable pictures of things in the world.

3 *(Example answer)* Road signs

2a 1 Calendar   2 Mechanical clock
3 Printing press   4 Telephone   5 X-rays
6 Television   7 Satellite

Focus on reading 1 *(p.105)*

1 See Student's Book page 217.

3 *-ing* clauses

A *making them far more convenient to use;*

C *replacing papyrus rolls; being both portable; Having remained dominant …*

E *Having originated … 1960s.*

-ed clauses

B *Invented in Germany in 1500; At first regarded purely as 'ladies' fashion' …*

E *… technology developed in the early 1960s …; Initially used only by scientists, …*

4 *(Example answers)*

1 He produced an essay *based* on information *downloaded* from the Internet.

2 The paper *containing* the results of the survey is about to be published.

3 The damage *caused* by the flood will take years to be repaired.

4 *Having finished* his speech, the President answered reporters' questions.

5 *Realising/Having realised* that he had lost the confidence of his team, the manager resigned.

Focus on reading 2 *(p.106)*

2 1 **iv** *Why they did this is still a mystery … 90,000 years.*

2 **vii** *Their only criteria are that a device must have been used …*

3 **vi** *(lukasa) … used to teach lore about cultural heroes … sacred matters*

4 **iii** *(missile mail) Sadly, the trial did not spark off a postal revolution.*

5 **xi** *It really depends on the society … power in society.*

6 **i** *Unfortunately, … that media can be murdered.*

7 **x** *… another feature of long-lasting media: they tend to be simple.*

8 **viii** *… many people … dead. I don't believe it for a minute.*

3 9 **E** *(paragraph E) many cities boasted … made up of underground pipes.*

10 **B** *(D) By learning the shapes … and the sequences in which they appeared.*

11 **G** *(F) These knots were tied by an official class … historians, scribes and accountants.*

12 **A** *(A) … present thinking is that … lunar calendar.*

13 **H** *(H) These attempts may vary … all based on the same simple idea.*

14 **D** *(E) Pigeon posts have been around for 4,000 years …*

15 **C** *(D) used to teach lore … designed to jog the user's memory.*

4 16 **B** *(paragraph C) Sterling and Kadrey set the ball rolling, but ultimately it is a communal effort …*

17 **D** *(G) quipu could have been taken a great deal further*

18 **A** *(A) … about 90,000 years. 'I doubt very much … will survive that long.' …*

Focus on vocabulary *(p.110)*

1 1 Take, for example, …

2 In the category … one group stands out …

3 … illustrate the point.

4 … to name but a few.

2 *(Example answers)*

1 The fact that many older people have no idea what DVD is **illustrates this point**.

2 Among these, **one** in particular **stands out**: the high costs of calls.

3 **Take, for example,** the dishwasher, which takes time to load and unload.

4 It is thought that they may not develop normal social skills, **for example**.

5 … the last hundred years, computers, lasers and fibre optics, **to name but a few**.

Focus on speaking *(p.110)*

1 Other possible factors include: cost (equipment, transmission), feedback (delayed or instant), security, written record?, pictures or documents?

14 ▶ The proper channels

TO SET THE BALL ROLLING ...

You could begin by doing an informal class survey to find out a bit about students' own preferences with regard to various media. For speed, use the Media survey (Questions 4–10) on page 114 as the basis for mini interviews. Point out the need to formulate suitable questions. (In the case of Questions 4–6, this may need clarifying beforehand.) Alternatively, devise a fuller questionnaire for discussion in pairs. Afterwards, ask a few students to report back on what their partner said.

Lead-in *(p.112)*

1 The example illustrates two typical features of text-messaging: the shortening of words, usually by leaving out vowels (MN = MAN, TCH = TEACH, etc.) and the use of numbers which sound like words (4 = *for*, 2 = *to*, etc.). If students are struggling to interpret the quote, ask them to try saying the first few 'words' aloud.

2 a These examples introduce an additional feature of text messaging: the use of letters which sound like words or parts of words (U = *you*, C = *see*, etc.).

   b If any students are unfamiliar with emoticons (emotional icons), sometimes known as 'smileys', explain that they are designed to look like facial expressions when viewed with your head tilted to the left. Ask why emoticons are needed in e-mail and other electronic messages, and establish that they are used to express humour or emotion where a message might otherwise be misinterpreted in the absence of vocal or facial expression.

3 You could help by telling students that four words have no silent letters. Let them compare answers before checking. Practise orally.

4 Practise the three sounds with more examples if necessary. To cater for varieties of English such as American English, you will need to include a fourth sound /æ/, as in *hat*. Explain that this sound usually replaces the British /ɑː/ in American English (though not in words with an *r* after the vowel, e.g. *hard, far, start*).

Again, you could help by telling students there should be <u>six</u> words in each column. Let students compare answers and practise orally after checking.

Focus on speaking 1
Communication problems (p.113)

If you have time, you could introduce this section (with books closed) by writing the following newspaper headlines on the board or overhead projector. Ask students to speculate about the story behind each headline, encouraging them to use appropriate language (*I think it might/could be about … It must be to do with* … etc.). NB The headlines match extracts A, D and B respectively.

> Parents pay for leaving children alone with TV

> E-mails spell disaster for English teaching

> When lessons interrupt an important call

1 Time students' reading strictly and let them discuss answers in pairs. You may want to look at some of the language in the extracts in more detail afterwards, e.g. A *Put simply, lone-viewing data;* B *fads, undermine, hence;* D *missives*.

2 These are fairly meaty topics, which should provide plenty of scope for discussion practice. Monitor the pairwork and make sure students are considering various aspects of the subject and using a good range of language.

Focus on listening 1 *Media survey (p.114)*

If you didn't use the survey at the *Lead-in* stage, give students a few moments to study the questions. Afterwards, you might want to focus on a few useful or interesting expressions from the recording script e.g. *many happy returns, I'm not terribly up on …, (it) bores me stiff, make a point of* (doing something), *(it) leaves me cold* (an informal expression).

KEY LANGUAGE
• **Topic vocabulary: the media**   Exercise 23, page 203

Focus on listening 2 *Couch potatoes (p.115)*

1/2 Let students read through the *Reminders* and study the diagrams in Questions 1–4. If they are weak in this area, you may want to spend a little time discussing the diagrams before they listen.

Afterwards, you might want to focus on a few useful or interesting expressions from the recording script, e.g. *a heavy viewer, to account for, news stroke factual, an interesting angle* (on a subject), *to be/feel left out, to be old hat* (familiar, old-fashioned, unexciting).

Focus on writing 1 *Dealing with different data (p.116)*

NB It's very important that students take note of the information in the *Exam briefing* on the weighting of each part in the Writing paper. In the exam, it's all too easy to get bogged down in Task 1 and find yourself with insufficient time to complete Task 2 satisfactorily.

Unless your students are very able, it's advisable to spend some time analysing the two graphs, and revising some useful language. One approach would be to ask a set of questions such as:

- What is the focus of each graph? (world news and local news)

- What are the main parameters? (percentage of people, time scale, media)

- Is there any difference in the ranking of the three media in the two graphs? (TV is the most popular source of world news; newspapers are **marginally more popular** than television for local news.)

- What is significant about the first graph? (Television is **by far the most popular** medium for world news; there has been **little change** in the relative popularity of the media over the period.)

- What is significant about the second graph? (There has been **a significant decline** in the popularity of newspapers and **a corresponding increase** in the popularity of television.)

- Compare the popularity of radio for world and local news, etc.

NB If students are having difficulty in selecting significant data in this kind of task, you could also prepare a set of sentences describing aspects of the graph and ask which should be included, which not (and why).

Focus on speaking 2 *The Internet (p.118)*

If you have time, you could extend Exercises 1 and 2 to include a discussion about various aspects of the Internet, e.g. the pros and cons of Internet shopping, the use and abuse of chatlines, the coming of e-books.

Focus on writing 2 *Beginning and ending (p.119)*

If necessary, revise the difference between the two approaches to essay structure, argument-led and thesis-led, before you begin. The exercises can be done either in pairs or as a class, but it would be useful to finish off with a round-up of key points.

Unit 14 Key

Lead-in *(p.112)*

1 Give a man a fish and you feed him for a day. Teach a man to fish and you feed him for a lifetime.

2 a 1 through 2 tomorrow 3 thank you 4 (I) will speak to you 5 See you later
  b 1 happy face: used when giving/receiving good news
  2 frown: bad news coming
  3 winking face: used when joking
  4 sceptical face
  5 shocked face

3 a through; gh
  b

answer	combat ✓	island	muscle
behind ✓	doubt	ignorant ✓	psychologist
calm	golfer ✓	knife	receipt
climb	half	listen	wrist

4 1 /ɑː/ calm, class, command, drama, half, past
  2 /ɒ/ quality, quantity, swallow, wander, watch, what
  3 /ɔː/ fall, law, raw, walk, warn, water

Focus on speaking 1 *(p.113)*

1 1 A television B mobile phones C e-mails D text-messaging and e-mails
  2 (*Example answers*)
  A The (harmful) influence of TV advertising on children B The problems of children using mobile phones in school C The stress which can be caused by e-mails D Teachers' concerns about the effect of text-messaging and e-mailing on spelling

Focus on listening 1 *(p.114)*

1 Matthews 2 21 3 full-time student 4 sports
5 (national) news 6 TV reviews 7 C 8 B
9 B 10 A

Focus on listening 2 *(p.115)*

1 New Zealand 2 Switzerland 3 C 4 B 5 B
6 C 7 A 8–10 A, D, F (in any order)

Focus on speaking 2 *(p.118)*

See Student's Book page 217.

Focus on writing 2 *(p.119)*

2 1 B 2 C 3 A
3 B
4 1 B 2 A 3 C

15 ▶ Beyond gravity

TO SET THE BALL ROLLING ...

Use the photograph on page 122 (or any other suitable picture on a space exploration theme) as the focus for a brief preliminary chat, to gauge students' interest and knowledge, and elicit some topic vocabulary. Try to steer clear of topics included in the Lead-in quiz, but if they should arise, avoid specific details.

NB The photograph shows Russian cosmonaut Valery Polyakov in the Mir space station, about to set the record for space flight. (See *Lead-in*, Question 7.)

Lead-in *(p.122)*

This warm-up activity allows students to share their knowledge of a few milestones in the Space Age and to speculate about some possibly surprising statistics. It also provides some background information for the Speaking topics which follow, and for the optional writing task (see *Focus on speaking* below).

Focus on speaking *The final frontier (p.123)*

1 Encourage students to make the most of these discussion points by giving detailed reasons for their opinions. After inviting brief feedback, clarify vocabulary as necessary, e.g. *blasted off*; *creaky* (informal expression meaning 'old and not in good condition'). You could also check other topic vocabulary such as *space suit, weightlessness* and *(zero) gravity* as a link to the main reading text.

2 Invite brief feedback afterwards and perhaps develop Question 2 into a whole-class discussion. It's possible that feelings may run high here, and opinions may polarise to some extent. If the discussion goes well, you may want to record some of the arguments on the board, as the basis for an optional writing task.

Focus on reading *Surviving in space (p.123)*

With books closed, ask students to guess how long they think a journey to Mars will take. Then refer them to the diagram on page 125.

1 Ask students to cover the text, apart from the headline and subheading. Invite brief feedback, and jot ideas on the board.

2 Set an appropriate time for skimming/scanning (say five minutes) and stick to it, to discourage intensive reading at this stage. Check results and compare with students' predictions.

3 Unless your students are at or near exam standard, allow a little time for them to find their bearings in this quite long text. Elicit ways of forming a general picture of the content (e.g. by **sampling** the text and/or by **skim-reading** and circling key topics in each paragraph). Make sure they study the *Reminders*, and if any students are struggling with particular questions, you may want to direct them to relevant areas of the text. Allow time for them to compare answers before checking.

For the True/False/Does Not Say section, review the distinction between False and Does Not Say answers if necessary, and use the checking phase to establish the difference very clearly. If students have had problems with Question 5, make a teaching point of the difference between *few* and *a few*, *little* and *a little* (see *Error Hit List*, Unit 16).

When checking the multiple-choice section, ask students to provide evidence from the text for their answers. Those who choose option B have failed to distinguish between long and short space flights, and this provides an opportunity to underline the importance of grasping the main issues in a text <u>and</u> reading the options very carefully.

Although the diagrams may look complicated, the task is straightforward once the relevant section of text has been found. This is where the initial text sampling or skimming that students have done should prove invaluable.

When matching opinions to experts, it may be helpful to work together to identify key phrases in one or two of the opinions and to ask for suggestions as to parallel expressions (e.g. 13: *prevent many deaths* = save many lives). Again, ask students to say which words/phrases in the text match the opinions.

NB The text contains a number of informal expressions which you could focus on if time allows, e.g.:

no worse for wear (also *none the worse for wear*) (lines 15–16) = unharmed by an experience. Compare: *He looked a bit the worse for wear after his all-night journey* = in a poor condition because of an experience.

an unknown realm (18–19) = unexplored territory. NB *realm* can also mean an area of activity, interest or study.

mere hiccups (61) = comparatively small problems. NB literally, a *hiccup* is a sharp repeated sound made in the throat, especially after eating or drinking.

bear fruit (86–87) = have a successful result

NB The text also provides an opportunity to focus on an important area of language: *-ing* forms and infinitives (see *Key language* below).

```
KEY LANGUAGE
```

- *-ing* forms vs infinitives
  Exercise 24, page 203

Unit 15 Key

Lead-in *(p.122)*

See Student's Book page 217.

Additional notes

6 Possible areas of confusion are: b) (*Soyuz* a series of Russian spacecraft), d) (*Voyager 1*, the US space probe and currently the most remote man-made object in space), and f) (the Hubble Space Telescope, named after the US astronomer, Edwin Hubble).

8 *Pegasus* was just five metres long. $10 million was the cost for each launch of the *Pegasus*. $300 million is the cost of a space-shuttle mission on a Low Earth Orbit.

Focus on reading *(p.123)*

3 1   F   *... more than two-thirds* (line 1)
  2   T   *... may gain 5 (five) centimetres* (13)
  3   DNS This may be true, but it's not mentioned in the text.
  4   T   *... polyethylene shielding will absorb the radiation* (64–65)
  5   F   Stress is caused when people have *few tasks* (78) and *little to do* (81). (See *Error Hit List* page 135.)
  6   DNS Again, likely to be true, but not mentioned in the text.
7–9 (in any order) A (e.g. lines 50–53)
     C (35–37)
     F e.g. with drugs (48–50); by making body parts (54–57)
10 coronal mass ejections
11 electrically charged gas
12 cosmic rays
13 E   *This technology has the potential to save ... lives* (99–100)
14 A   *These changes are the price of a ticket to space.* (23–24)

15 F   *The more research that's done .... everyone is going to be.* (111–113)
16 C   *Understanding their biological effects is a priority* (72–73)

Focus on vocabulary *(p.127)*

1   1 expansion
   2 adaptation; adaptor
   3 adjustment
   4 density
   5 renewal
   6 confinement
   7 survival; survivor
   8 investment; investor
   9 disturbance
  10 diagnosis
2   1 (the sense of) sight
   2 the sun
   3 space/the universe
   4 stars (+ planets, moons, comets, asteroids)
   5 the body (of living things)
   6 the heart
   7 the mind
   8 (the study and treatment of) diseases of the mind
   9 the stomach
  10 bones, joint and muscles
3   1 optical illusion
   2 solar eclipse/rays
   3 cosmic rays
   4 astronomical telescope
   5 physiological features
   6 cardiac arrest/surgeon
   7 psychological warfare/profiling
   8 psychiatric illness/hospital
   9 gastric ulcer
  10 orthopaedic surgeon/hospital

Focus on vocabulary *(p.127)*

1 Check spellings and clarify meanings as necessary.

2 Again, clarify meanings and practise pronunciation as necessary. Include additional adjectives relating to students' areas of study as appropriate.

16 ▶ Falling forward

TO SET THE BALL ROLLING ...

For speed, write prediction B from the *Lead-in* on the board, and ask students to guess who the speaker was, and say why this prediction was ill-advised. Ask for examples of everyday predictions (e.g. weather forecasts, political polls, predicted exam grades in school reports, star signs, if appropriate), and introduce a brief discussion of students' opinions as to the value (or otherwise) of such predictions.

Lead-in (p.128)

1 Ask students to work in pairs to answer Questions 1 and 2. Encourage them to say as much as they can about each subject, e.g. why Albert Einstein was very far from a failure, why prediction C was badly timed. In feedback, include some of the points from the Discussion notes and Example answer in the Key.

2 Give students time to study the picture and compare ideas together before opening up a class discussion.

Focus on speaking 1 *Predicting the future (p.129)*

1 Give students time to read through the predictions and check any unknown vocabulary before they begin. Make sure they are working together to discuss and categorise the issues, according to the instructions. Afterwards, discuss students' results and reasons, but avoid definitive answers which would pre-empt the listening task to follow.

2 Organise this activity as pair interviews for more direct exam practice. Afterwards, invite brief feedback, and perhaps develop one or two questions into a whole-class discussion.

KEY LANGUAGE
• **Expressing probability** Exercise 25, page 205

Focus on listening 1 *Reality or science fiction? (p.130)*

For extra support, give students time to look through the questions and perhaps discuss ideas in pairs. You could also talk through their predicted answers before the listening phase. Ask students to compare answers before checking.

Focus on writing 1 *Explaining how something works (p.130)*

Point out that when the topic is a technical process (rather than a natural one), it's often helpful to start by describing the basic layout and function of the equipment. It's worth practising some of the *Useful language* by giving students a few objects and/or systems to describe (e.g. *TV remote control, bicycle, parking meter, cash dispenser*).

Spot the error (p.131)

If you can make an overhead transparency of the language of probability from *Key language* Exercise 25, this will be a useful way of guiding the checking phase, and drawing students' attention to some of the key issues. Remind them to note down errors they make in correction so that these can be revised regularly and, hopefully, eliminated.

Focus on listening 2 *The techno-house (p.132)*

Read the advice in the *Reminders*, and let students study the diagram. Check their ideas, and discuss topic vocabulary, as appropriate. For extra support, allow time for students to study the remaining questions, and perhaps discuss predicted answers. Ask them to compare answers before the checking phase.

Focus on speaking 2 *Personal goals (p.133)*

This is an important topic area for both Part 1 and Part 2 of the interview. The activity gives students the opportunity to practise talking about a future goal and also to listen to fellow students' descriptions. If there is time, ask students to repeat the exercise with one or more different topics.

Refresh students' memories about mindmaps, if necessary using a separate topic (e.g. 'A person you'd like to meet').

Rearrange seating to facilitate group discussion (if possible), and check that students are clear about the instructions, have each chosen a different topic, and are equipped to keep time. Allow a couple of minutes for thinking/note-making.

Monitor students' performances, and note points for feedback.

Ask students to report back on what another group member said.

Use feedback to identify key points of a successful long turn, e.g. covering both the *describe* and *explain* elements, and using a good range of language. Invite students to mention examples from their groupwork to illustrate these points.

Focus on writing 2 *Summarising sentences (p.134)*

1/2 Read through the introduction and *Useful language*, drawing students' attention to the more impersonal use of *we* rather than *I*. Students may find it easier to work in pairs to complete Exercise 2.

3 Read through the *Reminders*, and revise the language on pages 68 and 69 if necessary. If students are still weak in this area of writing, have a planning phase in class, so you can discuss approaches and check paragraph plans, etc. You could also supply the following introduction:

Most people would agree that technology has transformed the way we live. But have all the changes been for the good? I would argue that …

With more able students, the topic would be suitable for timed exam practice.

Unit 16 Key

Lead-in (p.128)

1 1 (*Discussion notes*)

A Despite his poor school report, Albert Einstein's scientific work was to revolutionise physics in the 20th century. He was awarded the Nobel Prize for Physics in 1920.

B Despite the captain's faith in its supposedly unsinkable design, the passenger ship *Titanic* sank, with the loss of 1,513 lives.

C The first Moon landing took place just twelve years later in 1969.

D The first mass-produced personal computers were produced less than twenty years later, and computer ownership has been growing rapidly ever since.

E The telephone quickly proved to be a great success. Four years after its invention in 1876, there were 30,000 in use.

F The typewriter caught on quickly after its introduction and soon became indispensable in offices around the world, with portable typewriters for home use following.

G The first mass-produced car, the Oldsmobile, was produced a year later in 1901. It has been estimated that there are around 500 million cars in the world today (with one billion forecast for 2025).

2 (*Example answer*)

Predictions often extrapolate from the current situation, assuming that conditions will not change and technological development will imitate existing processes. In E–G, the assumption is that social conditions will remain stable. Cars will be restricted to the rich, who will employ chauffeurs to drive them. Labour will continue to be cheap, allowing companies to employ messenger boys, and communications will be local.

2 (*Example answers*)

• Private planes exist, but are so prohibitively expensive that only business corporations and the super-rich can afford them.

• Robots exist, but their main use is to carry out repetitive, predictable industrial processes. They are not yet sophisticated enough to cope with complex, unpredictable tasks around the home.

• This vision assumes the continuation of the nuclear family with Father as breadwinner, Mother as housewife. It fails to foresee a situation where both parents go out to work, and the woman may even be the main breadwinner. It also fails to foresee single-parent families.

Focus on listening 1 (p.130)

1 social (and) economic   **2** technology
3 into existence   **4** (About) half/50% of (the) /
(About) 3,000   **5** 4–6 (four to six) billion   **6** more
(and) smaller   **7** 2025   **8** political stability   **9** Japan
(and) Korea   **10** problem situations

Focus on writing 1 (p.130)

2 1 enables   **2** consists of   **3** called   **4** are used for

3 (*Example answers*)

1 Once the boat has entered the lock, the upper gates must be closed. Then the lower paddles are opened to allow the water to flow out. When the water in the lock reaches the lower water level, the lower gates are opened and the boat can leave the lock.

2 The procedure is reversed. Once the boat has entered the lock, the lower gates are closed. Then the upper paddles are opened to allow the water to flow into the lock. When the water in the lock reaches the upper water level, the upper gates are opened and the boat can leave the lock.

4 (*Example answer*)

When a boat needs to move to a lower water level, the upper gates are opened to allow the boat to enter the lock. Once the boat is in place, the upper gates close behind it, and paddles or valves in the lower gates are opened to let water out. The boat is then carried down as the water level falls. When the water level has reached the same height as the next section of canal, the lower gates are opened for the boat to pass through. When a boat needs to move to a higher water level, the procedure is reversed.

156 words (including introduction)

Spot the error (p.131)

1 ✓   **2** … you will probably fail …   **3** … there's a 90% probability …   **4** ✓   **5** ✓   **6** In my opinion/view
7 … a good/strong chance/a strong possibility …
8 ✓   **9** … unlikely that a new form of energy will be found …   **10** ✓

Focus on listening 2 (p.132)

1 C *demand for the house of the future is still very low*
(A – only in special show homes; B – the technology is *already in place*)

2 A *the thing they're mostly concerned about is location*
(B – most prefer *a traditional-looking house;*
C – *… not terribly interested in*)

3 B *a saving of twenty weeks on conventional construction*
(A – *save both time and money*)

4 grass   **5** glasshouse   **6** pond   **7** solar energy
8 Internet House   **9** office or car   **10** staircase

Focus on writing 2 (p.134)

2 (*Example answers*)

1 … the arguments in favour of co-educational schools.

2 … whether this is a good use of public money.

3 … we need to look at the counter-argument.

4 Given the costs involved, …

5 Having discussed some recent developments in teaching, …

6 Having looked at some of the arguments for reducing speed on our roads, …

17 ▶ Avoiding gridlock

TO SET THE BALL ROLLING ...

Find out who can drive, who plans to learn, etc., and follow this with a brief topic discussion, e.g. *What are the advantages/disadvantages of owning a car/riding a bicycle?* NB It's best to avoid going into issues covered in the unit in any depth (road safety hazards, safe vs dangerous drivers, traffic problems and solutions).

Lead-in (p.136)

2 Ask students to study Car 1 and elicit as many clues as possible about the type of driver (see the Key). They can then discuss the other driver types in pairs. Afterwards, broaden the topic by asking which of the driver types (if any) would be typical in students' own countries or cultures, and what other road safety hazards (if any) there might be.

3 Make it clear that students should consider the general driver types A–E rather than the specific characters illustrated. They will find answers to Questions 2 and 3 in the reading text. The answers to all three questions are shown in the table on page 212.

NB There is an optional Task 1 *Writing practice* related to this topic (see below), which includes practice in interpreting data. This task could be set before or after the reading text, as appropriate.

WRITING PRACTICE

- **Presenting and comparing data (guided practice)**
  Exercise 7, page 212

Focus on reading 1 *Smashing stereotypes (p.137)*

NB Although this text is shorter than a typical IELTS reading passage, it provides useful task practice.

1 Read through the *Task approach* and remind students about skimming and scanning skills if necessary.

2 Give students time to identify key words or phrases in the questions, and let them compare results. Check answers thoroughly, underlining the need for close textual analysis.

3 It's worth asking students to spell out the difference between the three possible answers once again. Although this may seem like overkill, this remains one of the trickiest areas of the Reading paper, and students need to be totally confident in tackling it. To reinforce these guidelines, check the answers thoroughly. Make sure students can identify the line number(s) and expressions which provide the evidence.

- **TRUE**: The statement contains the same information as the text, but may express this differently. *Look for synonyms, parallel expressions and summarising statements.*

- **FALSE**: The statement mentions information from the text, but this is inaccurate. *If you make the statement negative, it will be true according to the text.*

- **DOES NOT SAY**: The statement contains information which is not in the text at all. *Making the statement negative does not necessarily make it true according to the text.*

NB The use of *little* (as opposed to *a little*) is significant in Question 15, and also appears in line 35 of the text. This language point is covered in the *Error Hit List* in Unit 16 (page 135), and it's worth focusing on at the checking stage.

If time allows, you could focus on a few interesting expressions from the text, providing further clarification as necessary, e.g. *violations* (6) (e.g. *of human rights*); *anecdotal* (9); *geared to* (15); *nod off* (54) – compare *doze off; combat* (59); *addressed* (62).

Optional activity: Recognising cohesive devices. Remind students what a fundamental feature of written English cohesive devices are.

Find the words in the text and say what they refer to (line numbers are given in brackets).

1 otherwise (9)	4 It (19)
2 it (13)	5 those (30)
3 this (17)	6 such (32)

Answers
1 (that) women <u>are</u> beginning to drive as aggressively than men
2 the question (of whether, as drivers, women differ from men)
3 the increase in women drivers
4 age
5 accidents
6 (accidents) which take place in the dark

NB There is a checklist of common reference links and three practice exercises, which would provide useful revision (see below).

KEY LANGUAGE

- **Cohesion: reference links**
  Exercise 10, page 193

Focus on speaking *On four wheels (p.140)*

Depending on the time available, <u>either</u> ask pairs to select a topic and talk together for four to five minutes, <u>or</u> allot two topics per pair and allow ten minutes discussion time. Either way, ask students to summarise their conversations for the class.

Focus on reading 2 *Avoiding gridlock (p.140)*

NB This text contains a number of examples of American English spelling and vocabulary.

1 Give students time to answer Questions 1–3, and discuss ideas briefly.

2 For the matching task, remind students of the difference between tasks where questions summarise information in a section, and those where questions pick out specific information (as here), and let them read through the *Task approach*. When checking, ask students to justify their answers as usual.

If you think students need extra help with the sentence completion, ask them to suggest other ways of saying the phrases A–H before they begin the task. When checking, ask them to identify the relevant sections of text.

3 Check whether students remember how to go about a completion task like this. If not, refer them back to the *Task approach* on page 75. Let them compare answers before checking.

Focus on vocabulary *More or less? (p.143)*

Point out that synonyms are commonly used to avoid repetition within a text, and that this exercise focuses on alternative ways of expressing *rise* or *fall*. The important thing is to recognise the broad meaning, rather than the precise connotations of a word. For this reason, it's best not to spend too long differentiating between words during the checking phase.

NB As mentioned in the *Exam briefing* on page 140, reading texts may come from a variety of sources, including American English. For practice in British vs American vocabulary, see *Key language* Exercise 26.

KEY LANGUAGE

- **British vs American vocabulary**
  Exercise 26, page 206
  Suggested approach for classwork
  Ask students to cover the jumbled answers and identify any expressions they know or can guess, before matching the remaining items. This task checks some basic topic vocabulary and could be extended to include other useful items as appropriate.

Unit 17 Key

Lead-in (p.136)

1 1 A   2 D   3 E   4 B   5 C

2 *(Example answers)*

Driver 1 is seen as someone whose image is very important to him and who may be a fast and fairly irresponsible driver. He has quite a *sporty* car, which has been *customised* with *chequered* stripes on the bodywork. He likes to be seen and heard, as he drives with the windows down and loud music playing. Potential hazards: fast and/or aggressive driving, distraction when using controls on car music system, etc.

Driver 2 is presented as a *harassed* mother driving a *people-carrier* full of *rowdy* children. She's shouting at them over her shoulder to be quiet/sit still. Potential hazards: lack of concentration/distraction.

Driver 3 is seen as a steady, cautious driver, who is trying to concentrate on his driving while his wife sits alongside pointing out directions or possibly criticising his driving. He's in an older, sensible car with *roof-rack* stacked high. Potential hazards: insecure or excess load, distraction, slow reactions.

Driver 4 drives a small economy car, perhaps her first. She is using a wing mirror to apply make-up, which suggests that she leads a *hectic* life or perhaps that she is more concerned with her appearance than with her driving. Potential hazards: inexperience, lack of concentration, etc.

Driver 5 looks like a businessman or salesman. He's in a hurry to get to a meeting of some kind in his *company* car. Potential hazards: excess speed, distraction caused by using a mobile phone and/or consulting a map while driving.

3 1 E   2 A   3 C

Focus on reading 1 (p.137)

1 1 (they seek/to gain) independence (line 8)

2 women (drivers) (16)

3 age (18–20)

4 55 (33–34)

2 5 B (lines 39–41)

6 A (54–56)

7 C (49–51)

8 A (44–45)

9 B (25–27)

3 10 T (lines 8–11)

11 T (12–14)

12 F (29–31)

13 T (46–48)

14 DNS

15 F (59–62)

Focus on reading 2 (p.140)

2 1 G   2 B   3 I   4 F   5 D

3 6 E (Section C)

7 G (*the dispersal of species,* Section D)

8 F (*changes in urban design,* Section F)

9 B (Section G)

10 D (Section H)

4 11 global car fleet (Section B)

12 cars (*cars become essential,* Section C)

13 (Nearly/Almost) a million (Section D)

14 (a) watershed (Section D)

15 (air) pollution (Section E)

Focus on vocabulary (p.143)

A 1, 2, 6, 9, 11, 12, 13, 14

B 3, 4, 5, 7, 8, 10, 15

18 ▶ Wish you were here

TO SET THE BALL ROLLING ...

Discuss one or more of the following quotes and/or build up a mindmap for Tourism as a way of activating topic vocabulary and exploring various aspects of the subject: social/sociological, economic, ecological, etc.

- *The whole object of foreign travel is not to set foot on foreign land. It is at last to set foot on one's own country as a foreign land.* G.K. Chesterton

- *Vacation: cramming a year's worth of living into a period of approximately two weeks, in an attempt to relax from the rigours of work.* Rick Bayan, *The Cynic's Dictionary.*

- *A perpetual holiday is a good working definition of hell.* George Bernard Shaw

Lead-in *(p.144)*

1 Questions 1–3 establish some basic facts about the tourism industry which are relevant to later speaking and writing activities. After students have checked the answers, you could usefully develop the discussion a little, e.g.:

- *What makes the top three countries so popular? Are there any surprises in the top ten? Which countries might change position in/enter the top ten soon?*

- *What do you notice about the top ten?* (e.g. They're all rich, industrialised countries; there's a north/south divide.) NB You could mention that 80% of tourism is made up of nationals of just twenty countries.

- *What basic categories can the attractions be divided into? What is the incredible appeal of Disneyland?*

Questions 4 and 5 allow students some personal input on the topic. They provide a good opportunity for giving reasons and using cleft sentences such as:

The thing I'd most like to see is …
The main reason I want to go there is …
What attracts/interests me most is …

2 Read through and clarify the explanation, as necessary, and practise the sounds in the example countries. Let students compare answers before checking.

Focus on speaking 1 *Tourism (p.145)*

This activity provides plenty of scope for a discussion of the downside of tourism. When students report back, encourage them to mention any personal experience they have, and to speculate about reasons for tourists' insensitivity.

Ask them to comment on any differences between their answers and the results of the survey (page 218).
NB The negative effects of tourism on local communities in developing countries is a topic in *Focus on writing 1.*

Focus on listening 1 *Worldwide Student Projects (p.146)*

Once students have studied the questions, check that they're clear about the instructions and know how to use the letters in the 'period' column in the table.

Focus on writing 1 *Presenting the solution to a problem (p.147)*

Previous discussions should have provided plenty of material for this topic, which is suitable for timed exam practice or homework.

Focus on speaking 2 *Time off (p.147)*

These tasks cover the three parts of the Speaking test, and students could work through them for the experience of a full interview. In this case, explain the procedure carefully (e.g. one student will be examiner for the three parts before swapping roles) and decide who will provide time checks. Ask students to read through the reminders for each part first. Alternatively, you could deal with each part separately, giving feedback as appropriate.

Focus on listening 2 *The end of oil (p.149)*

When there are several task-types and a lot of detail like this, it may not be possible to study every question in advance. Ask students which tasks they think they should concentrate on and establish that they should study the **pie chart** (noting roughly how it's divided), and the **table** (especially the three headings (Questions 7–9).

Focus on writing 2 *Dealing with different data (p.150)*

As this is the last task focusing on interpreting and presenting data, it's a good idea to have a round-up of key advice. You could use the first part of each *Don't* as a prompt, and ask students to complete the advice, and you should also be able to elicit the main *Dos* with a little help. Two additional points of advice about discussing more than one diagram could be added (see page 116).

• Study each diagram carefully to get the overall picture.

• Be clear about what each diagram contributes to the subject.

Before students begin,

• draw their attention to the bar marked EU average and elicit or check expressions like *(well) above/below average,* etc.

• remind them about the need to vary expressions, e.g. *Britain, the British, Britons, British drivers, car use in the UK.*

NB There is an example answer in the Key, although there are many alternative ways of completing the task.

Unit 18 Key

Lead-in *(p.144)*
1 See Student's Book page 218.
2 1 eight, freight, grey, weigh
   2 buy, height, light, while
   3 freer, we're, sphere, year

Focus on speaking 1 *(p.145)*
1 See Student's Book page 218.
2 (*Example answers*)
• Tourist destinations could limit visitor numbers in any one year (as Bhutan does, for example).
• A tourist tax could be imposed to fund spending on conservation or infrastructure.
• There could be legal requirements that international developers protect or improve the local environment.
• International developers could be required to work in partnership with local firms, so that a proportion of the profits remains in the local economy.
• Tour companies should brief representatives and tourists better, particularly with regard to cultural and religious matters.

Focus on listening 1 *(p.146)*
1 international understanding **2** improvement
3 M **4** (very) basic conditions **5** L **6** 250
7 disabled **8** (a) passport photo
9 terms and conditions **10** 1/a/one month

Focus on listening 2 *(p.149)*
1 Credit **2** global warming
3 3,000 (three thousand) **4** transportation
5 industry **6** buildings **7** Mexico, former Soviet Union (*both ticked = 1 mark*) **8** Canada, Germany, Japan, USA (*all four ticked = 1 mark*) **9** India, South Korea (*both ticked = 1 mark*) **10** B

Focus on writing 2 *(p.150)*
(*Example answer*)
The graphs give information about methods of travel and commuting times for six European countries, as well as the average figure for the European Union. From the information, we can see that car use is highest in Denmark at about 12,500 kilometres per person a year, and lowest in Spain and Germany. Perhaps surprisingly, the Danish also make far greater use of alternative transport than people in other countries, travelling over 3,000 kilometres a year by bus, tram, metro or bike, which is more than double the EU average. By comparison, the British and French travel less than a third of that distance by public transport. When it comes to commuting times, British drivers spend about 47 minutes each day travelling to work, which is more than any other country. In Denmark and Italy, on the other hand, where many more people use public transport, commuting times are significantly lower.
(*150 words*)

19 ▶ Face value

TO SET THE BALL ROLLING ...

To revise some topic vocabulary, draw a simple face on the board and build up a mindmap around it, e.g. **features** (*chin, cheek,* etc.); **descriptions** (*round/oval shape, pale/dark complexion, unshaven/clean shaven,* etc.); **expressions** (*smile, grin, frown, glare,* etc.); and perhaps one or two **idioms** (*at face value, pay through the nose*). Keep this last section brief, as there's an exercise on such idioms in the *Key language* section (Exercise 27).

Lead-in *(p.152)*

It may help to agree one or two easy expressions (e.g. *happiness*) and leave students to work out the others. *Disgust* and *contempt* may well need clarification. It's worth drawing attention to certain facial features, but try to avoid discussing them in any detail, since this would impinge on reading tasks later in the unit. In Exercise 2, Question 3, discuss any interesting cultural differences.

Focus on speaking 1 *Face the facts 1 (p.153)*

Students will be able to compare their answers to these questions with information in the reading section to follow, so keep feedback to a minimum.

Focus on reading 1 *Face the facts 2 (p.153)*

1/2 Set a tight time limit to encourage the use of skimming/scanning skills, before checking answers to Questions 1 and 2 in Exercise 1. Let students read the extracts in more detail before discussing answers to Exercise 2.

3 This language area has been practised in earlier units and, if students haven't done so already, they could complete the tasks in *Key language* Exercise 10 as revision.

4 Make sure students are really studying the words in context, and ask them to compare ideas before checking. NB It's worth eliciting the noun from *collide (collision),* since this is tested in *Focus on vocabulary*.

Focus on reading 2 *Face (p.154)*

This is the last exam reading passage, so little additional support should be needed, apart from reading through the *Reminders*, and perhaps revising ways of forming a general picture of the text (e.g. by sampling). Allow students as near to the target exam time of twenty minutes as possible and be prepared to analyse answers in some depth afterwards.

Focus on vocabulary *(p.157)*

If time is short, these tasks are highly suitable for self-study, since Exercise 1 can be checked using a dictionary, and answers to Exercise 2 can be found in the texts, using the references in brackets.

KEY LANGUAGE
• **Idioms with *face*, etc.** Exercise 27, page 206

Focus on speaking 2 *(p.158)*

These tasks allow students to role-play Parts 2 and 3 of the interview. The two parts can be tackled separately, with both students discussing a Part 1 topic before moving on to Part 2. However, if the procedures are thoroughly familiar, and the Speaking test is looming, you might prefer each student to work through <u>two</u> parts before swapping roles.

1/2 Give students time to read through the *Reminders* and check that they are clear about the instructions. Divide them into pairs, allot initial roles and make sure they have some means of checking time. Once the interviews are under way, monitor to ensure that students are following the correct procedure, and note down points for feedback.

3 Remind students of the timing for this part of the interview (four to five minutes). It's important to include feedback on these discussions, so if time is limited, you could specify (or let students select) just two or three topics.

Unit 19 Key

Lead-in *(p.152)*

1 See Student's Book page 218.

Focus on reading 1 *(p.153)*

1 1 C   2 A   3 D   4 B

3 1 misunderstandings caused by the absence of body language and/or facial expression
   2 see the expression
   3 the facial movements previously mentioned (averted gaze, brief smile, etc.)
   4 defendants
   5 the child
   6 face-to-face communication (with parents and peers)

4 *(Example answers)*
   1 bump into each other
   2 likely (to)
   3 concise/using few words
   4 not sorry
   5 broken (of rules, laws)
   6 vitally/extremely important
   7 children of their own age
   8 response

Focus on reading 2 *(p.154)*

1 (It's) more mobile (para. B)
2 frontalis, risorius (in any order) (C)
3 at birth (C)
4 (the) nose (D)
5 lie detection (E)
6 Descend (C)
7 Rise and arch (D)
8 Retract(ed) horizontally (C)

9 Tighten (D)
10 straight down (H)
11–13 C, D, F (in any order) (H)
14 B (G)
15 C (I)
16 D (J)

Focus on vocabulary *(p.157)*

1 1 annoyance
   2 annoyed/annoying
   3 anxiety
   4 collision
   5 counterfeit
   6 counterfeit
   7 deceit/deception
   8 deceitful/deceptive
   9 emphasis
   10 emphatic
   11 existence
   12 existing/existent
   13 falsify
   14 falsehood
   15 honesty
   16 response
   17 responsive
   18 voice
   19 vocal/voiced
   20 widen
   21 width
   22 withdrawal
   23 withdrawn

2 1 into   2 In   3 at   4 in; for   5 in   6 on
   7 On; at   8 of

20 ▶ Through the lens

TO SET THE BALL ROLLING ...

Ask students to complete the sentence *A picture is worth a thousand ...?* (Answer: *words*) and discuss this common saying briefly, e.g. *Think of a situation when this is particularly true. Why are pictures so powerful? Do you prefer instructions to be in words or pictures?*

Lead-in *(p.160)*

1 When students have had a few moments' discussion in pairs, invite general feedback and ask for comments on the special qualities of each medium. Use this opportunity to find out if anyone is particularly interested in one of the media.

2 Make it clear that they should identify the general uses or categories of photography illustrated (e.g. formal portraits) rather than specific subject matter. Ask pairs to list uses and then team up with another pair and compare lists.

In feedback, ask students to suggest other related uses of photography (e.g. *formal portraits*: passport/identity card photos; *medical*: micro cameras which can travel through the body). You could also broaden the discussion to include other uses of photography including *aerial* (for map-making, weather forecasting, etc.), *education/training* (visual aids), etc.

3 Use the examples to remind students about *syllables* and *stress* and give brief practice. When checking, clarify the meaning of any unknown items, especially those relating to photography (e.g. *enlargement, negative, perspective, projector*).

Focus on listening 1
Photography courses (p.161)

Focus on listening 2 *History of cinema (p.162)*

You may prefer to play the two recordings consecutively without the interruption of the Film Quiz. In this case, let students discuss the quiz before the listening practice.

For Question 1 in the Film Quiz, note that although modern photography began in France in the 19th century, the development of the camera goes back much further, as students will hear when they listen to the recording.

Begin these last two listening practices with a round-up of key advice, e.g.:

- check how many **question-types** there are and read the **instructions** for each set;

- study the headings and lay-out of **tables** carefully;

- when you have to choose words from **a list**, think about the **pronunciation** in advance.

Focus on speaking *Practice interview (p.164)*

If you want to deal with each part separately, revise key advice beforehand, let each student practise their topic, and give feedback before moving on to the next part. Alternatively, students can work through all three parts before swapping roles and repeating the procedure. In this case, have a round-up of key advice for all three parts first, and make sure students know exactly what to do before they begin.

Part 1

- Listen carefully and make sure you answer the questions which are put (not a similar question you've prepared for!).

- Give full answers with reasons or examples, whenever possible.

Part 2

- Make brief notes, perhaps using a mindmap, to ensure you cover all the points on the topic card.

- This is your opportunity to demonstrate your fluency. Try to use a good range of vocabulary and structure, and to keep talking for at least a minute.

Part 3

- Don't be afraid to ask for clarification, e.g. *I'm not sure if I understand the question. Could you explain?*

- Give reasons and/or examples to illustrate your point of view.

- Remember to link your ideas (e.g. *not only ... but also ...; On the other hand, ...*).

Focus on writing *Describing an object (p.165)*

Read through the *Exam briefing* and give students a few moments to look at the instructions for the task and the diagrams of cameras. To allay any alarm, ask them to estimate how many words will be needed to describe each camera from the total of around 150. In fact, allowing for the introductory sentence, only a basic description of each is possible.

Let students read through the *Task approach* notes, and discuss Question 2. Check and practise *Useful language*, as necessary.

There is a gapped model answer for this question in the *Writing practice* section (see below), but students will benefit most if they attempt their own answers first. Elicit a few descriptions orally, encouraging students to make use of the expressions listed and to use alternatives for *was invented*.

Give students twenty minutes to complete the task. The gapped model and/or the additional writing topics (see below) can then be set for homework.

WRITING PRACTICE

- **Task 1: Describing objects (guided practice)**
  Exercise 8, page 213
- **Task 1: Describing objects (exam task)**
  Exercise 9, page 214
- **Task 2: Presenting and justifying an opinion (exam task)**
  Exercise 10, page 215

Unit 20 Key

Lead-in *(p.160)*
2 **A** advertising
 B amateur photography (holiday snaps)
 C news reportage (Greek athlete winning Olympic medal)
 D formal record/portrait
 E crime prevention/detection (photofit)
 F medical (X-ray)
 G crime prevention/detection (CCTV image)
3 **A** accessory, advertisement, photographer, technology, transparency
 B advertise, cinema, digital, negative, photograph
 C commercial, develop, enlargement, perspective, projector
 D landscape, portrait, programme, tripod, wildlife

Focus on listening 1 *(p.161)*
1 Foundation
2 2–4.30
3 16 weeks
4 YES
5 (at) any time/flexitime
6 60 hours
7 B, E (in any order)
8 A
9 B
10 B

Focus on listening 2 *(p.162)*
1 See Student's Book page 218.
2 **1** drawing
 2 entertainment
 3 one person
 4 projection system
 5 Train Robbery
 6 full-length sound
 7 (Disney) cartoon
 8–10 (in any order) cheap land (available), low wages, (incredibly) varied landscapes

Focus on writing *(p.165)*
2 (*Example answers*)
was introduced, appeared, became available

▶ Recording script

Unit 2, Focus on listening 1
Students' Union survey (p.19)

I = Interviewer; S = Student

I Hi, I'm from the Students' Union. **We're doing a survey of students' eating habits.** Is it all right if I ask you a few questions?

S Will it take long?

I No, not really. Five minutes maybe? There aren't all that many questions.

S And what's it for exactly?

I Well, we wanted to get an idea of the sort of things students eat on a regular basis, and find out how aware people are about diet and nutrition and things. **The idea is to produce an information leaflet about healthy eating.**

S Yeah, I suppose something like that'd be quite useful, a leaflet I mean, especially for new students. Anyway, what do you want to know, exactly?

I OK, first question. What would you say your favourite food is?

S That's easy. **A burger and chips. Lots of chips!** I must say I like a nice Chinese meal as well, and maybe spaghetti once in a while … But no, the best has got to be a burger.

I OK, and what's your least favourite food?

S Hm. Let me think. I've never been that keen on cauliflower. Or fish – the smell puts me off. But no, **the thing I really can't stand is salad.** Rabbit food, I call it. I know lettuce and things are supposed to be healthy and all that, but it's just not a real meal, is it?

I Mm. Tut tut. You're getting into some bad habits there, you know. Anyway, moving on … Let's take a typical day. How many meals do you have? I mean proper sit-down meals, not snacks.

S Well, I nearly always oversleep, which means I generally skip breakfast altogether. And then I'd probably just have a bar of chocolate for lunch. So in answer to your question, **I don't sit down to a proper meal till the evening.**

I OK. Typical student, I suppose! And the next question: How many eggs would you eat in a week? One? Two?

S Well, I don't do much cooking as a rule, but **every Sunday I make myself a nice fried breakfast as a treat. That's sausages, bacon and two eggs,** the works. Lovely!

I That sounds OK once a week. But I wouldn't recommend it on a regular basis. Too much fat. And how about fresh fruit? Does it figure in your diet at all?

S Naah, not really, well, I know it's bad, but … I'm just not in the habit really. I suppose **I might eat an apple once in a blue moon.** But that's about it.

I Pity. But I suppose it's better than nothing! And would you say you had a sweet tooth?

S I guess so. Well, most people have, haven't they? Me, I can't resist a bar of chocolate.

I OK, one more question: is eating healthily important to you at all? I mean, would you choose one thing rather than another because it was more healthy?

S No, I can't say that I would. I don't really think there's any difference in taste. **I think all this craze for organic food is rubbish. It's just a way to make money.**

I OK. Well, that's more or less it, apart from the last section.

I If I could just take a couple of personal details? Your name? It's not obligatory, actually …

S That's all right. I'm Jamie **Buckingham**.

I Is that Buckingham as in the palace?

S Sorry? Yeah, that's right. **B-U-C-K-I-N-G-H-A-M**.

I Mm-hm. Got that. And which course are you on, Jamie?

S **I'm doing a degree in Travel and Tourism.**

I Mm! Lucky you! That's in the Business Studies Faculty, right?

S Correct.

I And which year are you in?

S I'm in my second year. One more to go!

I Right, that's everything. Thanks a lot for your help.

S No problem. Cheers.

Unit 2, Focus on listening 2
Healthy eating (p.20)

T = Tutor; L = Linda Golding

T I think that's all I need to say at this stage by way of an introduction to the college. But just to round off the morning, we can turn to something different – a subject which I think is close to most people's hearts – food! So let me introduce Linda Golding, the college Welfare Officer – Linda …

L Thank you. Hello, everyone. Yes, I'm here to say a few words about healthy eating. And **the first thing I want to emphasise is the importance of a balanced diet.** The right balance is vitally important for health, both mental and physical, especially when you're studying hard or under stress. I know it's tempting to eat a lot of snacks and take-outs, but remember that they tend to contain a lot of sugar and fat. And we eat too much sugar. Did you know that in Europe and the USA, **we're eating about twenty times as much sugar as we did in 1800?** Shocking, isn't it? And also five times as much fat. No wonder there's been a huge increase in heart disease and other illnesses in the West. So in the short time I've been allotted, I'd like to run through some basic principles.

Now, one of the most important things to include in our diet is fresh fruit and vegetables. The advice is that **we should be aiming to eat five servings every day.** It sounds a lot, I know, but you soon reach that if you have a banana with your breakfast, an apple at lunch and three vegetables with your evening meal.

Secondly, most of us need to try and reduce our sugar intake. Remember that many processed foods and ready meals contain sugar. And the **one thing to be especially careful about is carbonated drinks like lemonade and cola.** They're usually packed full of sugar. So avoid carbonated drinks and choose water or fruit juice instead – it's better for you!

Another thing to watch is your fat intake. Most of the fat in our diet comes from meat and dairy products, so try and stick to lean meat, poultry and fish, and **make a point of choosing low-fat dairy products,** things like yoghurt or skimmed milk. Oh, and don't buy hard cooking fat – use sunflower oil instead.

Next, we all know that cholesterol is a bad word. It's found in meat and dairy products, of course, but don't forget that it's also in eggs. So **limit the number of eggs you eat to three or four a week.** That's what the health experts suggest.

Just a couple more points. Most of us eat far too much salt, and that can lead to high blood pressure. So **cut down the amount of salt you add to food.** When you're cooking, **try using lemon juice instead** as a way of enhancing the flavour.

Finally, don't be tempted to skip meals. It's much better for your health if you **eat regular light meals, three times a day,** rather than just one enormous meal.

Now, just for fun, here's a question for you. What do you think is **the world's most nutritious fruit?** An apple, would you say? Or an orange? Well, you may be surprised – it's actually **an avocado pear.** You know, those dark-green fruits you see in salads sometimes. Avocado pears contain about 165 calories for every 100 grams. That's more than eggs or milk.

They also contain twice as much protein as milk and more Vitamin A, B and C.

Well, that's all I have time for now. And, yes, it's lunchtime, so enjoy your meal and be healthy!

Unit 4, Focus on listening 1
Wasting energy (p.35)

T = Tutor; S = Susan; P = Peter

T Good morning, everyone. Now, whose turn is it to do their mini-presentation today? Peter and Susan? OK, what topic did the two of you decide on in the end?

S We thought we'd have a look at the problem of waste in cities.

T Fine, well, when you're ready.

S OK. One of the many problems about cities is that they create such an enormous amount of rubbish. I've got some figures here to show you ... Umm, how does this thing work?

P Press the 'On' button.

S Right ... well, as you can see from the graph, New York produces about fifteen million kilograms of waste a day. It's a world record ...

P But not exactly one to be proud of!

S No, and **Tokyo comes next with about eleven million.** Basically, the richer the city, the more rubbish it generates. The thing is that in developing countries, much more waste is recycled, so there's less to dispose of. If you compare Los Angeles and Calcutta, for example, they both have roughly the same population, but Los Angeles produces about ten million kilograms of rubbish, while **Calcutta, a much poorer city, only produces half of that, five million kilograms.**

P You forgot to mention Mexico City.

S Yes, Mexico City's huge, but it only generates about seven million kilograms – less than half the figure for New York. Now, the big question is, what do we do with all this rubbish? At the moment, most of it ends up on rubbish tips or buried underground, which is a terrible waste of resources.

S And there's another problem, which Peter will talk about. Over to you, Peter ...

P Thanks, Sue. Yes, the other thing is that it can take an incredibly long time for rubbish to biodegrade, that is, to break down and decay. Just to give you an idea, food and other organic material is the quickest to biodegrade. **A loaf of bread decays in about twenty days,** for example, as long as the conditions are right. We throw away tons of newspapers and packaging, and paper takes anything from three months to a year to biodegrade. But **the conditions have to be**

damp. In dry conditions, it can last for decades. Metals take even longer, obviously. Most, like tin or iron, can take anything between one and ten years …

S But that doesn't apply to aluminium, does it? And **80% of soft-drink cans are made of aluminium.**

P No, that's right. Aluminium's a special problem because it doesn't rust. So recycling is really the only answer. And **another major problem is plastics.** There are 80 different types, for a start. Scientists think a typical item like a bottle could take a hundred years to decay. But as plastic has only been around for about a century, we can only really guess. And the longest lasting of all is glass. We know from archaeological evidence that **glass can survive for at least 4,000 years,** and who knows, maybe longer?

S Thanks, Peter. Now, just to round off, I wanted to say a word about some of the factors which can affect the process of biodegrading. One is **temperature** – things decay more quickly when it's warm and more slowly in cool temperatures. Another factor is **humidity.** A moist environment speeds up decay. And the third is **oxygen** – that's a bit more difficult, because some materials, like oil, need the presence of oxygen to break down, while others don't.

T OK. Good work, both of you. Now, are there any questions?

Unit 4, Focus on listening 2
Case study: São Paulo (p.38)

Is everyone here? Good, well, last week we talked about the astonishing growth of the world's cities, if you remember, and today I want to look at some of the reasons for this. What is it that draws people to leave their homes and families and move to big cities? To answer this question, I'm going to take São Paulo in Brazil, as an example.

First, some basics. There's a fact sheet on São Paulo in your books, but I think it's slightly out of date, so let me give you the correct information and you can make any changes. OK? Well, the city dates back to the 16th century – 1554, to be precise. By 1970, it had a population of 7.8 million; not quite a megacity, but growing fast. I think your book gives the present population as 15.2 million, doesn't it? But **the most recent figure I have is 16.5 million**, which means the population has more than doubled since 1970. **That makes São Paulo the world's third largest city,** according to UN statistics. But other cities are growing even faster, and if UN projections are correct, by the year 2015, São Paulo will have fallen to the fourth largest city, after Tokyo, Mumbai (formerly Bombay) and Lagos in Nigeria.

São Paulo is South America's leading industrial city, and **two of its most significant manufacturing products are cars and computers**. On the agricultural side, Brazilian coffee is world famous, as you know, and **São Paulo is the country's main centre for the coffee trade.** Now, I hope you managed to get all that …

Now let's look at a survey which was carried out among migrants to São Paulo. These are people living in the 'favelas', or shanty towns, on the outskirts of the city, and the aim was to find out why they'd decided to leave their homes and move there.

One set of reasons for migration are described as 'push factors'. A typical push factor was that there had been a poor harvest, for example. Another was that **there wasn't enough money to make improvements to farms**, so old farms remained inefficient and uneconomic to run. Some migrants said that opportunities for education were very limited in the countryside. And others mentioned problems to do with the weather. The main reason given here was **floods. Floods** occur from time to time after heavy rain, and they **can cause terrible damage to farmland, homes and other property**.

Another set of reasons are 'pull factors', or factors which attracted migrants into the city. The main pull factor people mentioned was that **cities offered more variety of work**. Employment opportunities are obviously much more limited in the countryside. In addition, migrants mentioned that wages are much higher in São Paulo than they are for similar work in smaller towns and villages. Another pull factor mentioned in the survey was **entertainment opportunities,** things like cinemas, clubs and sporting events. And we all know how the Brazilians love football! People also mentioned the fact that there were **better hospitals and health facilities available in town.** Last but not least, some people said that if your relations already live in the city, it makes the move easier, because you have someone to help you settle in, find work, etc.

The survey also looked at 'migration obstacles', that is things which can stop migrants moving to the city. The main one here is a question of money. Unless you can walk to the city or hitch a lift, **you need to pay for transport. If you're poor, this can be a major stumbling block.** Secondly, members of your family may object to the idea of your moving away. And that, too, can be a difficult obstacle to overcome.

Well, that's all I have to say on the São Paulo case study, but if you're interested in following it up or finding out more about the city, there's a Reading List on this handout, which I'm going to pass round now …

Unit 6, Focus on listening 1
Student interviews (p.50)

R = Rob; L = Linda Richmond

R Hi, come in. Take a seat. We haven't met before, have we?

L No.

R I didn't think so. Well, I'm Rob, I'm one of the Student Counsellors here. And you are … ?

L Linda Richmond.

R Right. And which course are you on, Linda?

L **I'm doing Computer Studies**.

R OK. Now, the reason for this little chat is that we wanted to find out a bit about what students do when they're not studying. How you relax. What activities you do. Things like that. But in particular, we'd like to know if there's anything we can do to improve the facilities available to students. OK?

L OK.

R So, tell me, where are you living at the moment?

L **On campus**.

R That's good. At least you don't have to worry about commuting if you're on campus.

L No, but it can be a bit of a problem getting into town in the evening.

R I suppose that's true. Swings and roundabouts. But, tell me, do you belong to any of the student clubs?

L Yes, **I joined the Film Society when I first arrived**, and I probably go along two, three times a week. Movies are great – they take your mind off your work and everything.

R Good. And that's it?

L That's it.

R So what do you think of the facilities in general?

L They're quite good. In my opinion, anyway.

R Any suggestions for improvements?

L Well, **I think the one thing that's really needed is a new gym.**

R You don't think the current gym is adequate?

L The thing is, it's nowhere near big enough. You can hardly ever get to use it, except at eight o'clock in the morning maybe. And the equipment's out of the Ark. It really needs updating. No, a new gym would be fantastic.

R OK, and finally are there any other activities you do in your spare time?

L Mm. **I do quite a bit of cooking**. It's the best way I know of relaxing. My speciality is curry! I'm always playing around with new recipes.

R Great. That's been very helpful. Many thanks.

R = Rob; J = Jim Maybury

R OK, so could I have your name?

J **Jim. Jim Maybury.**

R Jim – er, sorry, how do you spell your surname?

J **M-A-Y-B-U-R-Y.**

R Maybury, thanks. And what course are you doing, Jim?

J Marine Biology.

R And how's it going?

J Fine, so far.

R Good, good, and where are you living?

J I've got a place five kilometres from college.

R Excellent. And student clubs, societies … Do you belong to anything in particular?

J Yes, **I'm a member of the Athletics Club**. We've just got back from an inter-university athletics tournament, actually.

R And how did you get on?

J We came second.

R Well done. That's quite an achievement. So you're obviously into sport. And what do you think of the university facilities?

J To be honest, **I think they're a bit limited**. Compared with other universities I know, anyway.

R I see, and what improvements would you like to see?

J **The number one priority, as far as I'm concerned, is a swimming pool.** I can't believe a university this size hasn't got one. It's crazy for students to have to go to the public pool in town.

R Yes, I must say you're not the first person to mention that. Actually, there is talk of a major fund-raising campaign for new facilities, so maybe there's hope on the horizon. Anyway, last question: Do you take part in any other activities? To relax or whatever?

J **I play the guitar mostly**. It's something I've always done and it's great for winding down.

R Terrific. Thanks, Jim. Good luck with the course.

Unit 6, Focus on listening 2
Ten ways to slow down your life (p.51)

We hear an awful lot about stress these days. There seems to be more pressure in everyone's life. So, is there anything we can do about it? Well, I think there is, and I'm going to suggest a few ways of slowing down the pace of life and making things a little less frenetic.

Let's talk about working hours first. Do you find yourself working later each day just to deal with your workload? The problem is that you'll be even less able to cope the next day if you don't give yourself time to relax. So, **my first tip is to set a finishing time, and then make sure you keep to it.** That's unless you have a real crisis to deal with, of course.

Next, what do you do at midday? Do you just eat a sandwich at your desk? Or, worse still, skip lunch altogether? Well, nobody can work efficiently for eight hours non-stop. So the next tip is to **give yourself a proper lunch break, I mean one that lasts at least 30 minutes,** and do try to get away from your desk, get some fresh air.

And what about all those messages which are waiting for a reply? Don't panic. **Start each day by putting things in order of priority. Deal with the most urgent e-mails, faxes or phone calls first.** The less important ones can wait. Remember, it's important to take control of technology rather than letting technology take control of you.

Now, do you suffer from clutter? I mean all the stuff that lies around on your desk because you don't know what to do with it. **Well, there's a very useful piece of equipment called the wastepaper bin.** And that's the best place for an awful lot of clutter. So use the bin for what it's there for. Be ruthless. You'll tackle the important things much more effectively with a clear desk.

It's important to be realistic. **You won't always be able to clear your in-tray by the time you leave.** But don't worry if there's still some work. The chances are that you'll be able to deal with the in-tray much more efficiently next day.

Remember: work should be fun. Really! But if you do find that things are getting on top of you, go and find someone to talk to. Only, don't talk shop. **Pick something to talk about that's outside work**, a football match, say, or a film. You'll feel much better, believe me.

OK, let's think about home now. The important thing when you get home is to forget about work. Don't go on about the awful day you've had. **Make a point of listening to other people** instead. Find out what's been happening in *their* lives.

And what do you do to relax in the evening? **The main activity for most of us, I'm afraid, is watching television.** The problem with this is that it's a passive activity. It won't recharge your batteries, and it won't re-energise you. **So give the TV a miss** and do something with your friends or family instead. That's far better relaxation.

Another good way to use your leisure time is to do something for someone else. After all, life is about more than making money or passing exams. **Why not get involved in your local community** in some way? You could lend a hand at your local school or old people's home, for example, or help raise money for a local charity.

And finally, why not take up a new activity? Maybe something you've always wanted to do, but weren't sure you were capable of. You could join a painting class, for example, or **take lessons on a musical instrument**. You could even take up a new sport like waterskiing. Why not? You might discover a talent you never knew you had!

And on that positive note, I think I'd better stop, and maybe if there are some questions …

Unit 8, Focus on listening 1
Music festival (p.65)

A = Andy; M = Maria

A Oh, good, Maria, I was hoping to catch you.

M Hi, Andy, what's up?

A Well, there's a group of us thinking of going to the music festival, and we wondered if you'd be interested in coming along.

M Sorry, what music festival?

A Didn't you know? There's going to be a big international music festival here with loads of famous names performing.

M I'm not really into classical music.

A Oh, it's not just classical music. There's all sorts. Just a minute, I've got the programme here. Yes, there's world music from an incredible variety of countries: Scottish and Irish **folk music**, for example, West African percussion, Russian choral music, which should be fantastic, Indian classical music – I could go on and on. And then if you're a **jazz fan**, there's **a special jazz weekend** and also a whole day of contemporary music.

M Any rock music?

A 'Fraid not.

M Still, it sounds interesting. When is it exactly?

A It's in May.

M Oh, I'm going to be away the first week of May. I don't get back till the 12th.

A Well, that's OK because **it doesn't start until the 9th** and we were thinking of going the following weekend, that's Saturday the 16th …

M Fine.

A Anyway, **it's on for a whole fortnight** so there'll be plenty of time to enjoy it.

A Look, let me tell you the things we were thinking of going to and you can say if you're interested in joining us.

M OK.

A Right, well, on the Saturday there's a talk about Cuban music – it's not only a talk, actually, there's a demonstration of all the different styles as well. **That's at half past ten in the morning** and tickets cost £6.

M Sounds great.

A And then in the afternoon, there's something called 'The sounds of Scotland' at two o'clock.

M I love Scottish music.

A Me too. **The tickets for that are £8.** And then, the next day …

M The Sunday?

A Yes. There's a fantastic band from The Gambia, who play all kinds of traditional music, and they've got a stunning lead singer, apparently. The concert's at seven o'clock in the evening and it's called **'Africa Alive'.**

M 'Africa Alive'.

A Yes, the tickets are £15 – they're a bit more expensive, because it's an evening concert, I suppose. What do you think?

M Yes, count me in, definitely.

A Great. Then, getting away from music, they're doing a special **cruise on a canal boat, including lunch** and also a talk about the canal and its history. It's on Sunday afternoon, and **it costs, let me see …. yes, £14.50.**

M I think that might be stretching the budget a bit too far!

A OK, well three out of four isn't bad! And then there are loads of other things going on at the same time as well. Art exhibitions and stuff. We liked the sound of **the Bus Stop Gallery.**

M The what?

A **The Bus Stop Gallery.** It's an art exhibition on a bus which tours around the country. Anyway, the bus is going to be at the festival, and we thought we'd go along some time.

M Why not? Look, shall I give you some money now?

A No, wait till I've got the tickets. By the way, students can get a discount on the price of the tickets, but **you might have to show your student card when you go in, so can you remember to have it with you?**

M Sure.

A Anyway, I must fly. See you.

M Thanks, Andy. Bye

Unit 8, Focus on listening 2
The Museum of Anthropology (p.66)
S = Sue; T = Tom Brisley

S It's time for our regular 'Museum of the Week' spot on the programme, and here's Tom Brisley to tell us about it. Where is it you've been, Tom?

T Well, I've just come back from Vancouver, Sue, and I must say I had a fantastic time. There's so much to see and do in the city. But if you get a chance to go there, there's one place you mustn't miss, and that's the Museum of Anthropology. It was certainly one of the highlights of my time in Canada.

The museum was actually established way back in 1949 and these days it's one of the most popular in Canada. It's worth going there just to see the building, in fact, because it's stunningly modern and dramatic – it's hard to believe it was built back in 1976. One very good thing is that **the museum's all on one floor,** which makes it easily accessible for wheelchairs. Another plus is that it's in the most beautiful setting, overlooking the sea. And inside, **you can see archaeological and ethnographical material from all over the world,** although what the museum is best known for is its collection of art and culture from the native people of the Pacific North-West.

It's not a large museum, so it's quite easy to find your way around. When you arrive, you come into an entrance lobby with **a small shop on the right,** where you can buy guidebooks and some interesting souvenirs. Then, if you walk straight ahead, you'll go down a sloping ramp until you come to a kind of crossroads with **an information desk.** It's worth spending a few minutes there, 'cos the staff are very helpful and you can pick up various useful maps and leaflets. If you turn left at this point, there's a large ceramics gallery, and if you turn right, you'll eventually come to the theatre. But instead, keep walking straight ahead in the same direction as the ramp and you'll find yourself in the museum's most impressive room, **the Great Hall.** This was designed to house 30 of the museum's largest totem poles and it's absolutely spectacular! The glass walls are fifteen metres high, and the whole design is based on the structure of the native wooden houses.

T After that, you can enjoy just wandering around the various galleries. Don't miss the Rotunda, which is the setting for a beautiful modern sculpture called 'The Raven and the First Men'. It's carved from a huge block of cedar wood and **it took five people over three years to complete.** One of the best things about the museum, by the way, is that nothing is hidden away in store rooms. Everything is on show in a fascinating section called 'Visible Storage'.

Now, a few practicalities. The museum is situated on the University of British Columbia campus, which is quite a long way out of Vancouver City, so **you'll**

need to take a bus to get there. Take a number 10 or a number 4 from town and stay on till the end of the line.

Finally, it's a good idea to check the opening times before you go. **If you visit in the winter, remember that the museum is closed on Mondays.** During the summer months, it's open daily. It's also worth noting that **there's late opening till nine in the evening on Tuesdays, and that's all year round.** If you want more information, the museum has a useful website, which you'll find on our Factsheet.

S Many thanks for that, Tom. And that report brings us to the end of the programme. And in next week's …

Unit 10, Focus on listening 1
Predicting a volcanic eruption (p.81)

S = Sarah; A = Alan

S Hi, Alan. Long time no see.

A Oh, hi, Sarah.

S You look busy. What is it? An assignment?

A Yes, on volcanoes. But I'm having a bit of trouble with it.

S We did that one last year. What's the problem?

A Well, I'm looking at ways of predicting when a volcano's likely to erupt, and I've come across this diagram …

S Looks interesting. Can I see?

A Sure. It's from a leaflet they give to local people in the Philippines and it shows the different signs to look out for. The trouble is, they're not all labelled.

S Mm. Oh, we can probably work out what the rest are. Let's have a go.

A Oh, OK, great. Well, starting at the top, there's that cloud of smoke or vapour or whatever, and it's at three different levels: high, medium and low. I assume that must be **the height of the cloud**.

S Yeah, I'd agree with that.

A Oh, right. But then we've also got 'strong', 'moderate' and 'weak' … I'm not sure. Could that be force, do you think?

S I wouldn't have thought so, no. That'll be **the volume of the cloud.** How large it is, basically. The bigger it is, the more likelihood there is of an eruption.

A Yes, that makes sense. Now moving down, we've got something labelled 'dome growth'. Dome, that's the top of the volcano?

S Right.

A Mm. And then 'ashfall'. Which is … ?

S See those little spots? I think you get particles of ash raining down.

A From the cloud, I see. Then up on the slope of the volcano, there's a tree or a bush or something …

S Yes, that'll be **drying vegetation**. As I remember, volcanoes give off an enormous amount of heat before they erupt, and that causes plants and trees and things to dry.

A I'm impressed. How do you remember all this stuff?

S Just my natural brilliance.

A Yeah, right. And then … what's that thing that looks like a hole in the slope?

S I think it's meant to show **a landslide**.

A Really? I'll have to take your word for that! I suppose it's not that easy to illustrate. OK, **landslide it is**. And then we've got, yes, must be rain …

S Well done!

A Thanks! … And a river of some kind. Would it be a river of lava? No, no, not before an eruption, surely?

S No, I think you'll find that's **mudflow**.

A Do you write that as one word or two?

S **Mudflow.** One word. They can happen before a volcanic eruption, as well as during, and if I remember rightly, they can travel at anything up to one hundred kilometres an hour.

A Wow! Really? You wouldn't want to get in the way of one of those, would you? OK, now what about these two little houses … They seem to be shaking. That's got to be **an earthquake,** right? Do you get earthquakes at the same time as volcanoes?

S Uh huh, I think the two things are very often linked, in fact.

A Right. Then there are things like, well, like little flowerpots … and a sign saying 'no water'. I guess they're wells. So, **wells … drying up!** What do you think?

S Yup, sounds about right for that one.

A Next there's a horse which looks as if it's going a bit crazy.

S Yes, that's a very interesting phenomenon. Apparently some animals can sense when there's a disaster coming, and they behave in strange ways. Dogs start barking, geese fly into trees, things like that. I think we can call it **'abnormal animal behaviour'**.

A Yeah, I remember reading about something like that in Japan. **Abnormal animal behaviour**. Got that. OK, next there are obviously some unusual sounds to listen out for.

S   Mm, before an eruption, you get **a rumbling sound**. Like thunder.

A   Thunder's bad enough – a volcano rumbling must be absolutely terrifying! Right, only one left now. And that's to do with smell, right? Quite an unpleasant smell, by the look of it.

S   Yes, volcanoes give off various gases, and one of the most obvious warning signs is **a sulphur smell**. It's pretty unmistakable.

A   **Sulphur**, phew, nasty. OK, well, I think that's it finally. Fantastic. You've been a great help, Sarah. Thanks a million.

S   No problem. But I'd better fly or I'll be late. Good luck with the assignment.

Unit 10, Focus on listening 2
Tsunami (p.82)

Good morning. Today we're going to look at natural hazards connected with the oceans. As you know, more than two-thirds of the Earth's surface is covered by water, and the main hazards, both at sea and along the shore, are caused by waves.

Now, waves can be measured in various ways. So first of all I'd like to clarify a few of the terms we need to use. If you could just turn to the diagram on page 82.

Right? Now, you see the waves running across the centre? And the sea floor at the bottom? OK. Well, **the highest point of a wave is called the 'crest'**. Remember the saying 'to be on the crest of a wave', to be very successful? Yeah? Then an important measurement: **wavelength, which is the distance between the highest point of one wave and the next**. Wavelengths can vary enormously, from a few metres to hundreds of kilometres, believe it or not. So far, so good. What else? Er, there's wave period, which isn't marked because it's a measurement of time. It's the time between one wave crest passing and the next. Then **the lowest point of a wave is known as the 'trough'**. Can you see that? That leaves wave height, which is a measurement of the vertical distance between the crest of a wave and the trough. And finally, depth, which, as I'm sure you know, is the distance between the mean sea level and the sea bed.

Right, well, most waves are produced by the effect of wind. But the most destructive waves of all are not, in fact, wind generated. These are the famous tsunami. The word 'tsunami', by the way, is Japanese for 'harbour wave'. **The majority of tsunami are caused by earthquakes** which occur under the sea bed, although a few are also caused by underwater volcanic eruptions.

Most tsunami – that's between 80 and 90 per cent – take place in the Pacific Ocean. This is because the majority of the Earth's earthquakes happen around that ocean in the so-called 'Ring of Fire'. **While they're in the open sea, tsunami waves are generally quite small, rarely more than half a metre high, in fact**. That usually surprises people. It's only when they reach the shore that tsunami waves reach such enormous heights. As a matter of interest, **the largest tsunami ever recorded was 64 metres high, that was in Russia** in 1737. It's also worth noting that tsunami have extremely long wavelengths. **In the Pacific Ocean, for example, the average wavelength is 480km**. This low height and long wavelength makes it difficult to detect a tsunami in the open sea. The deeper the water, the faster the tsunami travels, and in the Pacific, **they can reach speeds of up to 700km an hour**. In 1960, a tsunami generated by an earthquake in Chile reached Japan in only 22 hours.

Let's look at another example now, the 1964 tsunami which hit Crescent City in the far north of California. This was caused by an earthquake which happened in Alaska four and a half hours earlier. The first two waves only hit the area around the harbour, but the third washed inland for a distance of 500 metres. **It flooded 30 city blocks** and destroyed a number of small, one-storey buildings. Luckily, there'd been enough warning for people to evacuate the low-lying areas, close to the sea shore. But the city authorities learnt an important lesson, and they took steps to prevent the worst of the damage from happening again. They turned the main risk area into a public park, and relocated all the businesses on higher ground. Incidentally, this approach has also been taken in Hawaii and Japan.

Now, before we finish, I'd just like to look at one more hazard, storm surges …

Unit 12, Focus on listening 1
The golden rules of listening (p.97)

P = Presenter; F = Frances Stephens

P   … and now it's time for the first in a new series called 'Get the Message', which looks at communication skills and how to improve them. Here's Frances Stephens to present it.

F   Hello. I think we'd all agree that good communication is vital, whether it's at home, at work or in personal relationships. So what are the key communication skills and how can we improve them? I'll be trying to answer those questions over the next four weeks. We'll be looking at the skill of speaking and considering **how to express yourself clearly in a discussion**, for example, or how to make a good impression in a job interview. We'll also be thinking about writing, including how to write an effective letter of complaint and the uses and abuses of e-mail. And finally, we'll be examining gestures and other **aspects** of **body language**, and considering the effect this has on face-to-face communication. But today, I'm going to start by focusing on the skill of listening.

F Now, listening is a far more sophisticated skill than most people realise, and poor listening is a very common cause of breakdowns in communication, so you need to be aware of a few rules.

The first golden rule of listening is to stop talking. Because you can't listen carefully if you keep interrupting. **This is especially important when the situation is familiar,** when you're talking to a relative or friend, say. In situations like that, it's all too easy to assume you know what the person means and start working out your reply, instead of paying attention to what they're really saying!

Next, try to relax! Research has shown that **it's much more difficult to listen effectively if you're feeling at all tense and anxious.** So if you've been dealing with a tricky problem at work, for example, and you feel the tension building up, take a deep breath before you answer the telephone. Let your brain adjust first.

You also need to make the speaker feel relaxed, and the way to do that is to **show them they have your full attention.** Try to look interested in what they're saying. Don't look over their shoulder or start scribbling on a piece of paper. Of course, **there may be reasons why you want to make notes.** In this case, tell the speaker in advance and explain the reason. Say the notes are to help you remember exactly what they said. Blame your poor memory, if you like. This is important, because we often use facial expression to tell us how the conversation is going.

Next, be aware of any prejudices you have – personal, political, whatever. And **make a conscious effort not to let these views affect your judgement.** You may not see things in exactly the same way as the other person, but that shouldn't stop you from trying to understand their point of view.

It's important to realise that listening is an active process. To listen effectively, **you need to use not only reason, but also feeling.** That means trying to identify with the other person and putting yourself in their position. After all, **the point of listening is to understand the other person's point of view – not to win an argument.** If you can empathise with the speaker, you're much less likely to jump to the wrong conclusion.

And one final point: **remember to listen for what the speaker is *not* saying.** That sounds strange, I know, but very often what's missing from a conversation is at least as important as what's there.

Now, to discuss some of these points, I've got with me in the studio Brian Morgan, who's a psychologist, and Tessa Wade, who works as a marriage guidance counsellor for …

Unit 12, Focus on listening 2
Making the most of your memory (p.98)

Now, today we're looking at memory. How it operates, and how *you* can make the most of it. That's if I remembered to bring my notes with me. They're here somewhere … Don't worry, just kidding!

OK, let's take a look at how memory works. In order for you to remember something, your brain has to perform a number of operations. First, the information has to be encoded, that is, taken in and processed. Then the information has to be held until it's needed, which is **the storage system of the brain.** Finally, it needs to be retrieved so that it can be used.

Most of us have problems with our memory at some time or other, and the older you are, the more likely this is to happen. Exactly how your memory suffers depends on which of your brain's systems is most vulnerable.

Another distinction we have to draw is between **verbal** and **visual** memory. Think about finding your way in a strange town. You may prefer to take in information verbally, for example, 'Turn left at the cathedral', etc. On the other hand, you may absorb information better in the form of a mental picture. To make the most of your memory, you need to use all these different systems to the full.

Another way of improving memory is with a method known as PQRST. This is a way of linking something you're trying to learn to what you already know. In this method, the P stands for **'Preview'**, that is, glancing through the text before reading it carefully. Then Q for 'Question', R for 'Read' and S … anyone care to hazard a guess? Well, it stands for **'State'**, as in 'to make a statement'. And lastly, the T stands for 'Test'.

OK. Well, let's look at those five steps a little more closely. If you've got an article, say, to read, **the first thing to do is to look through it quickly,** without worrying about every word. And when you've done that, you have to ask yourself, 'What do I know about this topic already?' Only then should you read the article carefully. And when you've done that, you need to **review the contents.** That means thinking about how the contents relate to what you already know about the subject. Finally, you should make a habit of testing yourself about what you've read.

The brain also has another type of memory system, which is called 'implicit memory', and **this enables us to absorb information without paying attention to it.** Sounds good, doesn't it? But there's a catch. If this system is to work efficiently, **it's crucial that you don't make any mistakes** while you're learning. If you're trying to learn a long list of vocabulary, for example, you may guess a few wrong meanings, and then your memory is likely to end up holding on to those wrong meanings.

So, **the best approach is to only test yourself on what you know well**. If you learn a few words at a time and gradually build up the list, you'll learn better than if you try to learn 200 words all at once. Little and often is the rule.

Now, here's something that might interest you. There's been some research in California which suggests that living a life of luxury can make you more intelligent! Scientists divided a group of 24 mice into two groups. One group was kept in standard conditions with as much food and water as they wanted. The other group was kept in luxury with larger cages, comfortable bedding and tasty snacks. And after 40 days, **this second group of mice were found to have fifteen per cent more cell matter in the part of the brain that deals with learning and memory**. Makes you think, doesn't it?

So I'd suggest you go out and pamper yourself a bit before the exams! But seriously, I'd like now to look at some other research into the mechanisms of learning and memory …

Unit 14, Focus on listening 1
Media survey (p.114)

I = Interviewer; P = Philip Matthews

I Excuse me, have you got a few minutes to answer some questions?

P What about?

I I'm doing a survey about how people use the media, things like newspapers, television, computers, etc.

P I see. Well, OK.

I Can I start by taking a few personal details? Don't worry, it's completely confidential.

P Sure.

I First, could I have your name?

P Yes, Philip **Matthews**. That's **M-A-double-T-H-E-W-S**.

I **Matthews**. Right. Got it. And do you mind if I ask your age?

P No, that's all right. **I'm 21** – I'll be 22 next week, as it happens.

I Oh, many happy returns in advance!

P Thanks.

I And what's your occupation?

P I suppose I'd have to say **full-time student**. Is that an occupation?

I It certainly is! OK, now turning to the survey proper. Do you buy a daily paper?

P No. I usually get one on Saturdays, though.

I What's the first thing you turn to in the newspaper?

P That's easy, **the sports section**. Doesn't everyone? You've got to check on your team's progress, read the match report, haven't you? And after that, I generally have a quick look at the **news**.

I When you say 'news', is that local, national or international?

P Oh, I'd say **national news**. Not local. Nothing very exciting happens round here! And I'm not terribly up on international affairs.

I And are there any other sections you read regularly? Business, for example?

P No. You must be joking! Business bores me stiff, I'm afraid. Let me think. I might have a look at the Arts section once in a while, but not as a regular thing. I suppose the only other thing I make a point of looking at is the **TV reviews**.

I You watch a lot of TV?

P 'Fraid I do, yes. Too much, probably!

I Right. That's it for that section …

I Well, if we could turn to TV and radio now …

P Right.

I Is there any particular kind of TV programme you watch?

P Well, the news, obviously, and sport. **But mostly, I want to be entertained. I like a good TV drama.** Something with a strong plot that you can get involved in. I don't watch a lot of documentaries, to be honest, and most of the comedies and quiz shows – they leave me cold.

I And do you listen to the radio at all?

P In the mornings I do. I prefer it to breakfast TV. But that's about the only time.

I So **would you say you got most of your information from television**?

P **Yes, I suppose I would.** As I said, I don't go in for a daily paper.

I And finally, just a couple more questions. Do you use a computer?

P Yes.

I And what would you say you use it for mostly?

P Mm, that's a hard one. I mean, I use it for computer games, like everyone else. But I've been cutting down on that lately. I think at the moment **I probably use it most for typing up lecture notes and other coursework, like assignments.** I did once try to keep an account of my spending on it. But I didn't get very far.

I Do you have Internet access?

P Yes.

I How do you use that mainly?

P Well, it can be very useful for college work. I've found an awful lot of information surfing the Web. But **in answer to your question, I think I'd have to say e-mail.** It's just a great way of keeping in touch with friends, especially the ones I have abroad.

I How about online banking? Have you thought about that?

P Not while I've got an overdraft, no!

I Fair enough. OK, well, thanks very much for your time.

P Is that it?

I Yup. That's it.

P OK, well, cheers.

Unit 14, Focus on listening 2
Couch potatoes, (p.115)

T = Tutor; A = Amy; J = Jonathan

T Hi, Amy, Jonathan. Do sit down … OK, we're talking about the media today, and I think Amy, you were going to start us off …

A Yes. I found a couple of pieces of information on the Internet.

T Fine.

A OK, well one was a survey of television viewing habits, looking at heavy viewers in different countries …

T And a 'heavy viewer' is … ?

A Yes, sorry. It's someone who watches TV for more than two hours a day. Anyway, there were two countries where more than 50 per cent of the people were heavy viewers. The UK came top with 58 per cent, and **New Zealand wasn't far behind with 53 per cent.** Some of the other results were quite surprising, actually.

T For example?

A Well, I would have expected the USA to be high on the list, but it came quite far down, with 40 per cent. Other countries, like Germany, were much higher. And then **the country with fewest heavy viewers turned out to be Switzerland.** I would have guessed, maybe, Portugal.

T Thanks. Well, that's useful data. Anything else to report?

A Yes, I also found a breakdown of TV programmes shown in an average week. It's only for one channel, but it's probably fairly typical. There are basically two major areas which account for most of the time. One is news stroke factual …

T Sorry, what do you mean by factual?

A Documentaries, current affairs, things like that. And the other is drama stroke entertainment.

T OK.

A Well, **news and factual programmes take up just over a quarter of the week. But drama and entertainment is much more popular. That accounts for about half the week's viewing. And the remaining time – what's that? About another quarter, I suppose – is all the other things like sport, education, the arts, etc.**

T OK. You might want to try and get data for one or two other countries perhaps. Anyway, thanks for that, Amy. Now, Jonathan, over to you …

J OK, well, I was interested in how children use the media, and I thought I'd look at the kind of home entertainment equipment children have access to.

T That's an interesting angle. What equipment specifically?

J Basically, video recorders, CD players and satellite TV.

T Right.

J Well, **video recorders seem to be pretty well universal nowadays. Almost every home with children has one, and that's been the case for at least ten years.** On the other hand, **CD players used to be a lot less common, but there's been a steady increase in recent years, and now about two-thirds of families have one.** Then finally, **satellite TV – that was fairly rare to begin with, but again there's been a gradual increase and nowadays it's in about a quarter of homes with children.**

T That's useful data, good.

T OK, Jonathan, now what would you say is the most important medium for children?

J TV, definitely.

T Any thoughts about why that should be?

J Well, I suppose television offers a lot of things: excitement, relaxation, etc. And it doesn't make any demands. It's a passive activity. But probably **mostly because all their friends watch it, and they don't want to feel left out.**

T Good point. Amy, you have a question?

A Yes, do we know how much time children spend watching TV?

J I think it's about two and a half hours a day in Britain, more than most other European countries, anyway. I remember another surprising statistic was that **two out of three children in Britain have TVs in their bedroom.**

A Really, as many as that?

J Yes, but the good thing is … is that their parents know where they are.

A But not necessarily what they're watching!

T Jonathan, any idea how many children have access to a computer?

J Just a sec. Yes, in Britain at any rate, 53% of children have a computer in the home. But **only about a quarter have a computer actually in their bedroom.**

T Mm. That's still quite a significant proportion, though. Anyway, finally, did either of you consider books at all? Or are they just old hat these days?

A Well, judging by the kids I know, I'd say books were definitely out of favour. They seem to see books as **dull and boring**. The sort of thing your parents approve of, you know. **Not exactly fashionable** amongst your friends!

J Yeah, my younger brothers are the same. Reading books is **too much like hard work** compared with watching TV. If they want entertainment, they'd definitely watch TV rather than read a book.

T What a shame! Well, all you need to do now is to write a report on your findings. By the end of next week, OK?

Unit 16, Focus on listening 1
Reality or science fiction? (p.130)

J = Jack; H = Helen

J Hello?

H Jack? It's Helen here. Look this is just a quick call. I've found an article on the Internet that might be useful for that assignment you're doing. It's basically a science-fiction writer's predictions about the future.

J Great – I could do with some inspiration!

H Well, if you've got something to write with, I can run through them for you.

J Just a sec … Right, go ahead.

H OK. Well, the first prediction is **'Massive, rapid change'**. He says **it's going to affect just about every area of life, political, social, economic and so on.** That's in the first category, which he calls 'Definite'.

J So he's put the predictions in categories. Interesting. But does he mention any specific causes?

H Let me see … Yes. He says **the transformations will be driven by**, and I quote, '**the forces of demography**, which has incredible mass, **and technology**, which has incredible velocity'.

J I'm writing that down. Right.

H Right. There are three more in the 'Definite' section: 'More city dwellers' …

J I've got a lot on that already, actually, but tell me about the other two.

H OK, well, talking about animals, he says that at the moment **more species are being destroyed than are coming into existence.**

J Species … Yup. Got that. Next?

H And on languages, he says **there are about 6,000 spoken today. But about half of those aren't being taught in school any more, so they're bound to die out.**

J I must say I didn't realise it was as many as that.

H No. Anyway, the next category is 'Almost certain'. You've probably got most of these: 'Global warming … computers everywhere …'

J Yes, got those.

H … 'more people' …

J Yes, population explosion, etc. But just a sec. He doesn't give any up-to-date figure for global population, does he?

H I think so. Yes. Six billion – that was the figure for 2000, at any rate. He also asks the question 'How many people can the Earth support?' Apparently, **most estimates put the Earth's long-term capacity at four to six billion.**

J But we've reached that already!

H I know, scary isn't it? Anyway, the third category is 'Probable', and here we've got 'More countries' …

J That can't be right, can it?

H Well, he says **there's a trend towards more and smaller countries which is going to continue.** He points out that the Soviet Union broke into fifteen parts.

J Right.

H … 'longer lives' …

J Got that.

H … and the other one here is 'Alternative energy'.

J Go on.

H He says **the basic science and engineering for a new energy economy will be completed by 2025.** But he thinks it'll probably take most of the century for it to actually be implemented worldwide.

J I'm just scribbling that down … OK, next?

H 'Space exploration'. He says **the exploration of our solar system will continue,** with more probes, more satellites, etc. **But only as long as we have political stability.**

J Good point. I'd better mention that – 'political stability – key factor'. Right.

H And he also thinks **new countries will be involved. He mentions China, Japan and Korea.** OK?

J OK.

H Then the last category is 'Possible' with only two headings. One is 'Nuclear war' …

J So he's not optimistic about world peace?

H Not terribly. He mentions several causes for concern. Like the amount of nuclear know-how there is around these days. And the fact that **there are still so many problem situations in different parts of the world, which could end up in conflict.** But also just the sheer number of nuclear weapons in existence.

J How depressing.

H And then the last prediction is what he calls 'First contact', finding life on other planets, I suppose.

J I think I'll steer clear of science fiction. Anyway, all this has been a huge help. Thanks a billion, Helen.

H No problem. Bye.

J Bye.

Unit 16, Focus on listening 2
The techno-house (p.132)

Next, as part of our Continuing Education series, we take a look at the house of the future. In recent years, house builders have been keen to show the public what new homes could look like. And to demonstrate what's possible, they've built special show homes featuring all the latest technology and energy-saving features.

But although the technology is already in place to bring all these exciting innovations into people's living rooms and bedrooms, very few new houses actually include them. Why is this? Well, it seems that **public demand for the house of the future is still very low.**

It seems people are not terribly interested in environmentally friendly technology. According to the developers, the home buyer's first consideration is price. They're simply not willing to pay extra for the benefit of all the latest technology. After price, **the thing they're most concerned about is location.** They may want to be near a good school, for example, or close to the shops. The third main consideration is design. And it seems most buyers still want to live in a traditional-looking house.

That said, there are a few forward-looking designers around who are hoping to persuade British people to abandon their prejudices and choose something new. A group called the Integer Project is designing houses which are both intelligent and green. For them, state-of-the-art design doesn't have to mean expensive. Integer Project houses use lightweight materials and prefabricated panels, which save both time and money. A typical three-storey house will take only 28 weeks to build, and that's **a saving of twenty weeks on conventional construction.**

One of the buildings designed by the Integer Project is the so-called Millennium House. This incorporates a whole host of high-tech energy-saving features, including computer-controlled energy-efficient lighting and heating. But one of its most unusual features has to be **the roof, which is covered with grass.** This provides an effective form of insulation, but how you manage to cut it, I'm not sure! The building is actually designed as a house within a house. There's an inner box containing all the main rooms, and this is **surrounded by an outer glasshouse**, which provides a controlled climate where plants can be grown. The lower floor is below ground level, so it's sheltered by earth on three sides to prevent heat loss. And outside, **the water is collected from the roof in a pond.** The water from the pond can then be used for watering the garden, and there's also equipment for recycling organic waste.

Integer principles are actually being tried out in one house in a new development by Berkeley Homes. Here, heating and lighting are controlled by computers, and the water is recycled within the house. **Water for domestic purposes can also be heated by solar energy,** thanks to solar panels fitted on the roof. This house is going to be the subject of ongoing research as to the benefits of its design and construction.

Another developer, Laing Homes, has teamed up with a firm of Internet experts to build a five-bedroom show house near London, which is called **the 'Internet House'**. From the outside, the house looks much like any other family home. But inside is a fascinating computer brain. The technology also allows a homeowner **to operate the heating, the TV, the security system and even the garden watering from the office or car using a website.**

A third developer, Redrow Homes, has taken the brave step of building 'The House for the Future', which can be seen at the Museum of Welsh Life near Cardiff. The most unusual design feature here is that **the staircase can be moved.** By changing the position of the staircase, you can alter the shape and size of the rooms as the family grows, and lifestyles change. The house is also extremely environmentally friendly, with facilities for recycling both water and waste.

'The House for the Future' provides a fascinating glimpse of what the future holds. The museum is open Monday to Friday …

Unit 18, Focus on listening 1
Worldwide Student Projects (p.146)

Hi, everyone. My name's Sam Thomas, and I'm here to give you some information about Worldwide Student Projects, or WSP for short. The talk takes about five minutes, and after that I'll be happy to answer questions, OK?

Right, well, WSP is a voluntary service organisation, which was **set up to promote international understanding.** Right now, we've got people from 30 different countries working in local communities around the world. So, if you're interested in joining them, I'd like to tell you about some of the opportunities that are available.

Now, depending how long you want to be away, there are three sorts of project to choose from: short-term projects lasting two to three weeks, medium-term projects lasting between one and six months and long-term projects which can be anything up to a year. One of the short-term ones we've got on offer at the moment is in Japan. **It's a village improvement project,** and the work involves clearing the river banks and planting flowers, things like that. You'd be working alongside local people, so you need a basic knowledge of Japanese for that.

The next one to tell you about is a children's holiday centre in Poland. What's required here is basically manual work. You'll be painting rooms, gardening and generally preparing for the children's arrival. **It's a medium-term project** lasting six weeks, and there's comfortable accommodation on site.

And now something for the animal lovers amongst you. It's a conservation project for sea turtles in Mexico. Sea turtles are under threat from poachers in that part of the world, so your main job would be collecting and moving the eggs to a safe site. It's a short-term project, and you'd be staying in a local school, but be aware that **it has very basic conditions.** Don't expect any luxury or satellite TV!

Now, here's an exciting opportunity in China for any budding architects. **This is a long-term project,** and placements are for nine months. You'd be working in an office in Shanghai, involved in planning and design, under supervision of a local architect. Oh, and I should mention that **you have to pay an additional fee of 250 US dollars when you arrive.**

Finally, do we have any medical students here? Because there's a placement available in **a centre for disabled children in India.** You'd be providing general medical care and also assisting in the outpatients department. It's for six months, so you can get plenty of experience and also do something worthwhile for disabled children.

Well, that's just a taste of the incredible range of projects we have to offer, but I hope it's whetted your appetite. And in case you do decide to apply, let me tell you what happens next.

First of all, you need to fill in an application form and send it to us. Oh, and **you should also include a passport photo,** by the way. Once we've received the form and photo, we process them and then we send you a 'Welcome' pack containing general information about the programme, together with the **formal terms and conditions.** These **terms and conditions** are basically a list of responsibilities on both sides, yours and ours – what happens if you want to leave early, etc. And you also get a detailed questionnaire, which helps us identify a suitable job for you.

Then, **about one month before you leave,** you'll receive all the details about your particular placement. And I think that's about it. Oh, I nearly forgot to mention, we've also got a website. The address is in our brochure. Now, are there any questions?

Unit 18, Focus on listening 2
The end of oil (p.149)

T = Tutor; A = Andrew

T Well, as I say, Andrew, we were a bit worried about your progress last term, but you've done some very good work recently, and I think it's fairly safe to assume you'll pass the course now. **In fact, if you can keep up this standard, we could very well be looking at a Credit.**

A A Credit? Really?

T Yes, as long as you keep up the good work. It's a real pity about last term, because you could have got a Distinction if you'd really wanted to, you know. Anyway, the other thing we need to talk about is your next assignment, right?

A Right.

T And you wanted to look at the subject of oil.

A Yes, it's a pretty major issue. I mean, there are millions of buses and cars and trucks in the world, all dependent on oil, and then the airline industry is carrying more and more people around the world every year, so you have to consider global warming …

T Hang on a minute, **I wouldn't go into global warming if I were you.** That's a huge subject in its own right, and quite a controversial one, I might add. **The assignment is only supposed to be 3,000 words,** remember. If you're not careful, you'll be writing a 30,000-word thesis!

A OK.

T Don't be too ambitious and keep an eye on the number of words. You've got a word count on your computer, haven't you?

A Yes.

T Good. Now, let's start with a few basics. Do you know how much energy is actually used for fuel, compared with other things?

A Yes, I found a breakdown. It's here somewhere … ah, yes, **transportation, that accounts for about a quarter of world energy.** Quite a bit less than industry, but it's still a significant proportion.

T **And what is the figure for industry,** as a matter of interest?

A **That's almost 45 per cent.**

T And the rest?

A **The other 30 per cent or so goes into buildings,** for things like heating and air conditioning, etc. But anyway, the main point I wanted to make was that we can't go on relying on oil for ever.

T So, Andrew, you think oil is running out. Have you any evidence of that?

A Yes, and it's quite frightening. Apparently, nowadays oil companies are only finding one barrel of oil for every four we actually use. Britain's North Sea oil is just about at its peak now. It'll start to decline pretty soon. And several major oil producers are already producing less …

T For example?

A Well, **the former Soviet Union is** a good example, and **Mexico** is another. Apparently even Saudi Arabia will reach its peak in a few more years.

T Interesting. OK, and do you know which countries use the most oil?

A Yes, a third of all the world's oil goes to North America. Worst of all is **the USA,** which gets through 459 gallons of gasoline per head every year, and **Canada** isn't far behind, with 303 gallons. Quite a long way after that comes **Germany** and then **Japan.**

T All fairly predictable, I suppose.

A Mm. But the thing is, there are other countries catching up fast, especially in the Asia-Pacific region. The two fastest growing are **South Korea,** which has doubled its use of gasoline in ten years, and **India,** which is up 64% in the same period.

T Good, that's all very useful data. Now, I suppose the other thing you need to look at is possible solutions. Any ideas?

A I haven't really got that far yet …

T OK, well, it comes down to two or three things, doesn't it? Persuading people to use less oil …

A By putting a tax on it, you mean. But that can penalise the poor.

T … or discovering new oil reserves somewhere in the world.

A Unlikely, and even that would only be a stop-gap. No, **I think the only realistic long-term answer is to find a replacement for oil.** I've seen hydrogen mentioned as a likely candidate.

T OK, well, I think we'd better leave it there. You seem to have a lot of useful information already, and you just need to work out the last section. And don't forget the word limit!

A I won't. Thanks for the help.

Unit 20, Focus on listening 1
Photography courses (p.161)

W = woman; M = man

W Department of Art, Design and Media. Can I help you?

M Yes. I'd like some information about photography courses.

W Let me just get the prospectus … OK, well, we do several different courses. I'll just run through them for you. The first is 'Introducing photography'. That runs for ten weeks and **it's a Foundation-level course,** so it's for people just beginning in photography.

M Right.

W That's on Monday evenings, from six thirty to nine thirty. Next, there's 'Black and white photography', which is at Intermediate level, so you would need some previous experience for that one. And you also have to have an interview with a tutor beforehand.

M Sounds interesting. Which evening is it on?

W It's a daytime course, actually. **From two to four thirty** on Tuesdays. That's also for ten weeks.

M That's a pity, I work on Tuesday afternoons.

W There's also 'Landscape photography', which is on Tuesday evenings, from six thirty to nine. That's a longer course than the others, **it runs for sixteen weeks.**

M And do you need previous experience for that one?

W Let me just check … Mm, it's Advanced level. So yes, you would, yes, and again **you'd have to be interviewed beforehand.** OK? Then the only other one we do is 'The art of digital photography'.

M I'm not sure that's for me, but which evening is it?

W **It's a Flexitime course.** It's on a Wednesday, but **you can do it at any time to suit you during the day.**

M How many weeks is that?

W It's up to you, really. **You have to do 60 hours in all.** And again, there's an interview.

M Right.

M OK. Can I just go back to the first course you mentioned. Um, what sort of things does that cover?

W 'Introducing photography'? Let's see what it says in the prospectus. Yes, here it is: 'Find out about different types of camera and camera care, **learn how the camera's controls operate,** and which lenses to use for different subjects, **study the main elements of effective composition'.** That's all it says. You could always talk to the tutor if you wanted more information.

M It sounds a bit … basic, to be honest. What about 'Landscape photography', was that the next one?

W Yes, that includes a field trip, where you go out with your tutor on location. But, look, to save me reading everything out, why don't I send you the prospectus?

M That'd be great. But could you just give me an idea of the fees?

W I'll just have to check … Right, 'Introducing photography', that's … yes, £95. 'Black and white's' the same, I think … No, I tell a lie, it's a bit less, actually, **£85**. And then 'Landscape' and 'Digital', they're both £140.

M Gosh. That's a bit steep, isn't it?

W Well, they are longer courses, if you remember. With the 'Digital', the fee also includes some photographic materials. And with the 'Landscape', **the cost of that field trip I mentioned is included.**

M Right. Oh, and I forgot to ask, is there an examination?

W Not as such. But you can have your work assessed and get a certificate if you pay a small extra fee.

M I see. Just one last question. How soon would I need to apply?

W Well, there are still places on all the courses at the moment, but they do tend to fill up quickly. 'Introducing photography' is always popular – we're running two courses this year so we can meet the demand. And 'Digital' is getting quite popular too. But **there are only twelve places on the 'Black and white' course**, so that everyone has access to the equipment. **If you're interested in applying for that one, I wouldn't leave it too long, if I were you.**

M I'll bear that in mind. Thanks very much for your help.

Unit 20, Focus on listening 2
History of cinema (p.162)

Right, if everyone's here … What I'd like to do in this first session of the Film Studies module is to take a brief look at the development of cinematography and pick out a few landmarks along the way. OK?

Now, the history of moving pictures begins with the camera, obviously. And the history of the camera goes way back to the 11th century, and something called the 'camera obscura', which was used in Arabia for observing solar eclipses. Over the centuries, **the camera-obscura principle was developed into a tool for drawing**. But this had serious limitations as a camera, because there was no way of actually fixing the image.

Then from the 17th century, we have the so-called 'magic lantern', which is really the forerunner of today's film projector. This began life as a way of showing scientific pictures, but because it could tell a story, **the magic lantern became most widely used for the purposes of entertainment,** and in the 19th century some very elaborate and expensive models were developed.

The first instrument which showed naturally moving pictures was the so-called 'Kinetoscope', nicknamed the 'peep-hole machine', and this was patented by Thomas Edison in 1894. The disadvantage with this was that **the film could only be seen by one person at a time.** So, although it was a great step forward, the Kinetoscope never achieved great popularity.

And then, around the year 1895, we reach the beginning of cinematography proper. It was in that year that **the Lumière brothers showed off the world's first projection system** to an audience in Paris. Incidentally, the film they screened with the new system showed a train approaching a station, and apparently it was so realistic that some of the audience ran out of the building in terror. All the same, the movies had been born.

As time went on, directors experimented with different kinds of film. One of the biggest successes of the early years was also **the first Western film ever made. This was a film called *The Great Train Robbery***, shot in 1903, and it paved the way for the careers of the great cowboy heroes like John Wayne.

As you know, the early films were silent, and usually accompanied by piano music. There were a few short experimental sound films during the early twenties, but **it wasn't until 1927 that the first full-length sound film was produced. This was the famous *The Jazz Singer*,** starring Al Jolson. At first, the film industry saw sound in films as just a gimmick which wouldn't last, but *The Jazz Singer* was so successful, they had to think again.

The final piece of the jigsaw was the arrival of Technicolor. **This was first seen in a cartoon made by Disney in 1932.** However, colour movies were expensive and difficult to produce, and it was 30 years or so before they completely replaced black and white.

Now, a word about the studios. The American film industry originally grew up on the east coast, in New York and Philadelphia. But filmmakers needed more reliable weather, and in 1910, many of them headed west for California. Now, why California? Well, apart from all-year-round sunshine, they found **plenty of cheap land** available where they could create studios and build houses. Another attraction was **the low wages** for all the various workers they needed to make films. And California also offered **incredibly varied landscapes** for every type of movie.

So directors and film stars poured into the little town of Hollywood, and the population expanded by an incredible 700 per cent in just ten years. And in no time at all, the name 'Hollywood' meant just one thing: movies.

IELTS Practice Test

Section 1

S = Sam; A = Anna

S Redland 254 319.

A Hi, Sam. Anna here. Have you got a second? I need some advice.

S Sure. What can I do for you?

A Well, I've put my name down for a college trip to Morocco and I know you've been there a few times …

S Yeah, great place. Which part are you going to?

A We've got a couple of days in Marrakesh, then we drive over the High Atlas mountains and head for the desert.

S Fabulous. When are you going?

A The second week of November. Till the 17th – **ten days in all**. What d'you think the weather'll be like?

S November … Well, it should have cooled down by then, fortunately. It can be incredibly hot in summer. Yeah, it should be very pleasant, around twenty degrees centigrade during the day, I should think. And there's not much likelihood of rain then. But **make sure you take something warm to wear – because the temperature can drop a lot at night, down to five degrees or even lower.**

A Really? Oh, that's worth knowing.

S But it's a wonderful time of year to go. There could be snow on the mountains by then. If so, the views'll be fantastic.

A Do you think we'll get to meet the people?

S Yes, if you stop in a village or go to a local market, the people are usually very friendly.

A Great. Now, I also wanted to ask you … **we've got the chance of doing this camel trek in the Sahara,** but I'm not so sure about it …

S **What? Are you crazy? It'll be the experience of a lifetime!** Think of it … riding through the desert, sleeping under the stars!

A But it's the riding bit I'm worried about. I mean, it's a long way to fall off.

S Where's your spirit of adventure? I'm telling you, you have to do it.

A OK, OK, you've made your point!

A Now, I need your advice on what to take with me.

S All right, well, it sounds as if there's going to be a lot of travelling, so think comfortable. Loose trousers, old T-shirts. Don't take anything new you haven't worn in yet. And that applies especially to shoes. Have you got some **walking shoes?**

A Yes.

S Good, you're bound to do a fair bit of walking. And a sun hat is absolutely essential, of course. But **if I were you, I'd take a warm jacket as well.** As I said, it gets pretty cold at night, especially in the desert.

A Right.

S **The other thing you'll need for the night in the desert is a sleeping bag.**

A Yes, you don't know anyone who could lend me one, do you?

S You can borrow mine if you like.

A That would be great. Thanks.

S Now, you're going with a group, right?

A Yeah, ten of us and an experienced leader.

S Good, well, there'll be medical supplies for the group, but **you should also take a small personal first-aid kit** with any special medication you need, plus painkillers, antiseptic cream, etc.

A Right.

S What else? Don't forget sun cream, obviously. And **I'd also take a small torch,** if you can. The electricity can be a bit unreliable in some places, and there won't be any in the desert! So a torch can come in handy. Those are the main things.

A You haven't mentioned a water bottle.

S Oh, I wouldn't bother if I were you. I've never had any problem finding drinking water in Morocco. It would just take up space and be an unnecessary expense. But one thing I nearly forgot – **make sure you take a camera.**

A I'd better check that mine's in working order.

S Yes, you'd kick yourself if anything went wrong with it. And **it's best to take all the film you need** with you as well. It's not that easy to come by outside the big towns.

A Right. Well, that's not such a long list. You've been a big help, Sam. Thanks a million.

S No worries. Have a great time!

Section 2

T = Tutor; S = Sarah Matthews

T OK, well, thanks everyone for coming. Our speaker today is Sarah Matthews. Sarah's a physiotherapist and she's going to give us some advice about healthy computing. Over to you, Sarah.

S Thanks, Simon. Now, I imagine that anyone who works on a computer fairly regularly has the odd backache or neckache from time to time. Well, you shouldn't ignore symptoms like that, they can lead to more serious problems.

There's a condition which has been in the news a lot recently, called Repetitive Strain Injury or RSI. It's usually associated with computer operators, but actually it can affect anyone who spends a lot of time working in one fixed position. **Factory workers are an obvious example**, because there's very little scope for movement when you're working on a production line. And **shop assistants can also suffer from RSI**, especially if their work involves repetitive tasks like filling shelves or operating the till. But **there's another group you may not think of immediately and that's musicians.** They're also at risk because of the repetitive movements they make.

It's not that easy to be precise about the number of people who are suffering from RSI, but **a recent study suggested that around 500,000 workers in the UK are affected.** And of course that means not only discomfort for the employees concerned, but also lost production for their employers.

S   And, of course, there's a cost to the economy as well. I'm not sure what the figure would be, but I do know that the number of disability claims relating to RSI has gone up dramatically in recent years. **Back in 1990, the percentage of total disability claims was just 1.7 per cent, but by 1998, this had gone up to 22.5 per cent. So almost a quarter!** And it's a trend that looks set to continue.

So what causes RSI? Well, what happens when you stay in one position for any length of time is that you're only using part of your body. That means that **certain muscles and ligaments aren't moved or stretched.** As a result, they tighten up, and this leads to problems. It's a very painful condition and it can take months of rest to recover from it.

And is there any way of avoiding these problems? Well, first of all, try not to spend too long on any one task. If you've got a lot of typing to do, try to take a mini-break every ten minutes or so. Just look away from the computer and move your shoulders, arms and wrists. Then **every half hour, you should take a longer break away from your desk**. Go and have a cup of coffee, make a phone call or just stretch your legs for a few moments.

Other things to think about: well, first and foremost you need a chair that provides proper support for your lower back. If it's adjusted to the right height, your feet should rest comfortably on the floor and **there should be no pressure on the underside of your thighs.**

The desk or table you work at needs to be the right height too. When you're using the keyboard, your forearms should be roughly horizontal, and **your wrists should be straight.** Avoid bending them up or down. And to minimise stretching, have the keyboard immediately in front of you, and any documents you need within easy reach.

Lastly, take good care of your eyes. Don't have the computer monitor near a window or lamp, because this can cause reflections. And make sure the screen isn't too bright or too dark. **Use the control on the monitor to adjust the brightness to a comfortable level.** And remember to keep the screen clean!

If you do think you're developing a problem, stop doing whatever it is that causes pain. Go and see a doctor straightaway, because early treatment is the key to success.

Well, that's all there's time for. I hope what I've said has been useful. And I wish you all healthy computing!

Section 3

P = Presenter; J = Jeremy Sandford; C = Caroline Clark

P   Hello. With me in the studio to discuss the future of work, I have Jeremy Sandford, who's an economist ...

J   Hello.

P   ... and Caroline Clark, who's one of a new breed of home-workers.

C   Hi.

P   Now, a report published last week says we can all look forward to working much shorter hours in future. Forgive me for sounding sceptical, but haven't we heard all this before? Jeremy ...

J   Well, it's true the labour market is still pretty traditional at this point in time, but in ten or twenty years, we'll definitely see some massive changes.

P   Such as? Can you give us some examples?

J   Well, **by 2020 there will be a lot more people on temporary contracts.** We estimate that the number of temporary workers will rise by twenty to 25 per cent. The idea of a job for life is already a thing of the past, of course, and people are going to have to become even more flexible. We also believe that there will be fewer people working in traditional office surroundings, and that **around 50 per cent of workers will be working from home in some way.**

P   Like Caroline here?

J   That's right.

P   But how do you know these changes are on the horizon?

J   Well, we did a survey of 200 companies, and 60 per cent said they thought there would be significant organisational changes in the next ten years. If that many companies are expecting change, I think we have to take the idea very seriously.

P   Right.

J   And also a lot comes down to statistics. We know, for example, that **there won't be enough young workers by 2020.** That's because of the falling birth rate in

Europe. At the same time, with better health care, better nutrition and so on, people are living much longer. That means that more than half the adult population of Europe will be over 50 before long. So obviously that'll create a gap in the labour market.

P Well, I suppose that could mean more opportunities for oldies like us, Jeremy! But what about the workplace of the future? **Are we really going to see the so-called paperless office?**

J **Yes, I think we are.** Filing cabinets full of documents will be a thing of the past. What we'll have instead is electronic screens which have all the characteristics of paper.

P Caroline, you're shaking your head …

C Personally, I don't see the paperless office happening. Not until we start changing habits in schools.

P OK. Let's turn to you now, Caroline. You work a three-day week, is that right?

C Yes.

P And what made you decide to leave a full-time job and work from home?

C Well, basically I felt **I wanted the time to do other things, apart from work. I wanted the chance to enjoy a few leisure activities, for example.** And I think a lot of other workers feel the same as me these days. Single mothers, for example, who want more time for childcare.

P Mm.

C And also **I used to spend two hours a day travelling to and from the office by bus. And commuting is quite stressful,** obviously, especially when the bus is late or there's some big hold-up. So **avoiding that is another big advantage.** And I also feel I can be more productive at home, because **you don't get so many distractions.** In the office, the phone's ringing all the time, and there are visitors and meetings.

P And is there anything you miss about your old job in the office?

C Yes, **you do feel a bit isolated sometimes.** In a funny way, I miss the coffee break and the chance to chat to colleagues.

P So workers of the future may end up missing the office, Jeremy?

J Well, I think the office will still exist, not so much for processing information, as it is now, but **mainly so you can meet other people.** There will always be times when a face-to-face meeting is better than a telephone conversation or an e-mail. And it's also important to make the point that flexible working doesn't necessarily mean working from home. **You'll be able to work anywhere you choose, really, so long as you have your laptop computer** and somewhere to plug it in.

P So it's definitely not the end of work as we know it?

J No.

P Well, on that reassuring note, my thanks to Jeremy and Caroline. Next week, we'll be discussing the future of the motor car …

Section 4

This is the first of a series of lectures on historic engineering structures. Today, we're looking at the Clifton Suspension Bridge in Bristol, which we hope to visit later this term, and I'd like to begin with a brief word about the bridge's history and about bridge building in general.

Now, people have been building bridges since prehistoric times. Over the centuries, bridge design has evolved using a variety of engineering techniques, but the objective has always been the same: to get to the other side.

One of the most basic types of bridge is the arch, and **there's evidence from the Middle East that people knew how to construct arches using stone or brick as early as 3200 BC.** The stone arch had the advantage of being quite simple to build, and it remained the main type of bridge design from Roman times until the early 1700s.

Another type of bridge with a long history is the suspension bridge, where the road is suspended from cables hanging between towers. **The first suspension bridges were simple affairs, made of rope and wood, and the earliest recorded examples were constructed around 550 AD in China.** But rope has limited strength, and it only became possible to build longer bridges when iron became available. The first major iron suspension bridge in Europe, completed in 1826, was the Menai Strait Bridge in Wales.

The story of the Clifton Suspension Bridge in Bristol began just three years later, in 1829. At that time, the city authorities wanted to build a bridge over the River Avon. **In order to choose the best design, they organised a competition,** and the winner, announced in 1831, was an engineer by the name of Isambard Kingdom Brunel. Work began the same year, but was almost immediately interrupted when serious riots broke out in the city. As a result, investors lost confidence, and work stopped until 1836. The two supporting piers had been completed by **1843, but unfortunately, at this point the money ran out, and work on the bridge came to a halt** for a second time. Then, in **1851, all the ironwork for the bridge was sold off in order to pay back the creditors,** and the project seemed to have reached an end. However, in 1860 there was a stroke of luck when a suspension bridge in London was demolished. That bridge had chains which were almost the same as the ones designed for Clifton, and **these chains were available to buy.** Events moved quickly after that. Money was raised, and work went ahead again in 1862. The bridge was finally completed amid great celebration two years later, in 1864.

We'll be examining some of the design features in more detail in the second half of this talk. But just as a footnote to this section, it's worth looking ahead to the future, and a couple of proposals for 'super bridges' linking not river banks or even countries, but continents.

One of these is for a bridge between Alaska and Siberia, which would be six lanes wide and 80 kilometres long. The water of the Bering Sea beneath is only about 50 metres deep, but **the biggest challenge is the extreme cold** of the location. This would restrict construction to five months a year and also close the road during winter.

There's a different obstacle facing a second proposal, a bridge linking Europe and Africa across the Straits of Gibraltar, **and that's the depth of water.** Although it's only 28 kilometres across, the water is as deep as 1,500 metres in places. In such deep water, a bridge may not be able to support its own weight, so engineers are considering using bridge structures which have never been attempted before.

A third seaway that engineers hope to cross in the near future is the Straits of Messina, between the island of Sicily and mainland Italy. Unlike the other two proposals, the Messina Bridge only involves one national government, and **the distance is relatively short at two and a half kilometres,** so there's a good chance it will be built. In this case, it's just a matter of who will provide the cash!

OK, let's take a break at this point and then ...

Practice test answer key

Listening

NB All spellings must be correct unless otherwise stated.

Section 1 (Questions 1–10)
1 A
2 B
3 C
4 walking shoes
5 warm jacket
6 (a) sleeping bag
7 (a) first-aid kit
8 (a) (small) torch
9 camera
10 film

Section 2 (Questions 11–20)
11 factory workers
12 shop assistants/workers
13 musicians
14 500,000
15 C
16 B
17 B
18 no pressure
19 straight
20 (the) brightness

Section 3 (Questions 21–30)
21–24 B, C, D, G (in any order)
25–27 C, E, F (in any order)
28 isolated
29 meet other people / have meetings
30 (laptop) computer

Section 4 (Questions 31–40)
31 3200
32 rope; wood
33 China
34 competition
35 money ran out/finished
36 (back) (the) creditors (*crediters* is an acceptable misspelling)
37 chains
38 extreme cold / (very/extremely) cold location
39 depth of water / (very) deep water
40 2.5

Academic reading

Reading passage 1 (Questions 1–12)
1 (coloured) minerals
2 (chemical) technology / science
3 (Ancient) Egyptian
4 technological innovations
5 B 6 C 7 C 8 G 9 D 10 B 11 A 12 F

Reading passage 2 (Questions 13–25)
13 G   14 C   15 I   16 B   17 E
18 planting weeds
19 Mexico
20 compost
21 pesticide use / use of pesticides
22 (teams of) oxen
23 (average) calorie intake
24 soil(s)
25 income/earnings

Reading passage 3 (Questions 26–40)
26 computer models
27 floods; droughts
28 eradication
29 (winter) freezing
30 excessive heat
31 T *floods and droughts … remain viable and hatch in still water*
32 T *climate change … predators that normally keep mosquitoes in check.*
33 DNS
34 F *The increased climate variability … more important than the rising heat itself.*
35 F *These urban dwellers*
36 organic matter
37 mosquito predators / predators of mosquitoes
38 birds
39 July heatwave
40 puddles / breeding areas

Academic writing

Task 1

MODEL ANSWER

The chart provides a breakdown of employment in a number of tourism-related industries over a ten-year period. Overall, we can see that the total level of employment increased by about twenty per cent during the period. However, there was some variation in the figures for the individual sectors. For example, while the travel industry increased its workforce substantially over the decade, there was relatively little growth in that associated with hotels and other tourist accommodation.

Travel represented the biggest area of expansion, having almost doubled its number of employees by 1999. The food industry also saw a significant increase, from 283,000 employees in 1989 to 357,000 in 1999, while the sports industry enjoyed an almost equal level of growth. The least successful sector was culture, including museums and art galleries, where the figures actually fell slightly over the period.

The data suggests that, despite minor fluctuations in the various sectors, employment in the tourism industry as a whole will continue to grow.

(162 words)

Task 2

MODEL ANSWER

Unemployment causes many problems for society. Individuals suffer not only economically, but also in terms of their self respect and even health. Inevitably, when the breadwinner is unemployed, other family members become victims too. Young people without job prospects may turn to drugs or crime to escape boredom and poverty. For all these reasons, any measures which can reduce unemployment are to be welcomed.

The first priority for the job seeker is information, and here the Internet offers a unique tool. Details of job vacancies and training schemes can be accessed within minutes on a computer screen, saving time and money that would otherwise be spent visiting employment agencies or buying newspapers. In addition, the Internet can be very useful in preparing for job interviews.

Once a suitable job vacancy has been identified, it's vital to respond quickly, and in this respect it can be argued that a mobile phone is more convenient than a conventional phone. Since calls on a mobile can be very expensive, however, costs can easily get out of hand unless they are monitored carefully.

It has to be said that, like any tools, the Internet and the mobile phone are only as good as their user. Both need to be used effectively, and of course both are open to abuse. There is little point in making technology available, therefore, without providing basic training in using it.

In conclusion, I believe there are strong arguments for giving unemployed people access to the Internet. However, the case for providing mobile phones is less convincing, and it may be more cost-effective in the long run to invest in relevant training programmes.

(273 words)